45

STUDY GUIDE

Conflict and Tension in Asia, 1950-1975

AQA - GCSE

app
available

Published by Clever Lili Limited.

contact@cleverlili.com

First published 2020

ISBN 978-1-913887-44-5

Cover by: United States Army Center of Military History on Wikimedia Commons

Icons by: flaticon and freepik

Contributors: Donna Garvey, Marcus Pailing, Shahan Abu Shumel Haydar

Edited by Paul Connolly and Rebecca Parsley

Design by Evgeni Veskov and Will Fox

DISCOVER MORE OF OUR GCSE HISTORY STUDY GUIDES

GCSEHistory.com and Clever Lili

AQA - GCSE

STUDY GUIDE

Elizabethan England, c1568–1603

GCSEHistory.com

26

AQA - GCSE

STUDY GUIDE

Conflict and Tension between East and West, 1945–1972

GCSEHistory.com

27

AQA - GCSE

STUDY GUIDE

Germany, 1890–1945: Democracy and Dictatorship

GCSEHistory.com

28

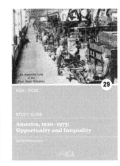

AQA - GCSE

STUDY GUIDE

America, 1920–1973: Opportunity and Inequality

GCSEHistory.com

29

AQA - GCSE

STUDY GUIDE

Britain: Power and the People, c1170 to the Present Day

GCSEHistory.com

30

alth and the People, e Present Day

25

England, c1066–c1100

35

AQA - GCSE

STUDY GUIDE

Conflict and Tension: The First World War, 1894–1918

GCSEHistory.com

36

AQA - GCSE

STUDY GUIDE

Russia, 1894–1945: Tsardom and Communism

GCSEHistory.com

43

AQA - GCSE

STUDY GUIDE

America, 1840–1895: Expansion and Consolidation

GCSEHistory.com

38

AQA - GCSE

STUDY GUIDE

Conflict and Tension: The Inter-War Years, 1918–1939

GCSEHistory.com

41

AQA - GCSE

STUDY GUIDE

Britain: Migration, Empires and the People, c790 to the Present Day

GCSEHistory.com

44

THE GUIDES ARE EVEN BETTER WITH OUR GCSE/IGCSE HISTORY WEBSITE APP AND MOBILE APP

GCSE History is a text and voice web and mobile app that allows you to easily revise for your GCSE/IGCSE exams wherever you are - it's like having your own personal GCSE history tutor. Whether you're at home or on the bus, GCSE History provides you with thousands of convenient bite-sized facts to help you pass your exams with flying colours. We cover all topics - with more than 120,000 questions - across the Edexcel, AQA and CIE exam boards.

GCSEHistory.com

 GET IT ON Google Play

 Download on the App Store

Contents

In this study guide, you will see a series of icons, highlighted words and page references. The key below will help you quick establish what these mean and where to go for more information.

Icons

 WHAT questions cover the key events and themes.

WHO questions cover the key people involved.

WHEN questions cover the timings of key events.

WHERE questions cover the locations of key moments.

WHY questions cover the reasons behind key events.

HOW questions take a closer look at the way in which events, situations and trends occur.

IMPORTANCE questions take a closer look at the significance of events, situations, and recurrent trends and themes

DECISIONS questions take a closer look at choices made at events and situations during this era.

Highlighted words

Abdicate - occasionally, you will see certain words highlighted within an answer. This means that, if you need it, you'll find explanation of the word or phrase in the glossary which starts on **page 109**.

Page references

Tudor *(p.7)* - occasionally, a certain subject within an answer is covered in more depth on a different page. If you'd like to lea more about it, you can go directly to the page indicated.

Conflict and Tension in Asia, 1950 - 1975 is a wider world depth study that investigates international relations. The course focuses on the causes and course of the Cold War in Asia. It considers why conflict occurred in this region, as well as how it developed, and why it proved difficult to find a resolution to the tensions. The course examines the roles of key individuals and groups in influencing change, and how they were impacted by international affairs.

Purpose
This study will help you to interpret the intricacies and diverse interests of different individuals and states. You will investigate themes such as capitalism and communism, international diplomacy, the causes and impact of warfare, and the challenges of bringing an end to war. This course will enable you to develop historical thinking, to identify and analyse causation and consequence, and encourage you to critically question sources.

Enquiries
Conflict and Tension in Asia, 1950 - 1975 is split into 3 key enquiries:

- Enquiry 1 examines the conflict in Korea.
- Enquiry 2 examines the escalation of the conflict in Vietnam.
- Enquiry 3 examines the ending of the conflict in Vietnam.

Key Individuals
Some key individuals studied on this course include:

- Ngo Dinh Diem.
- Dwight D Eisenhower.
- John F Kennedy.
- Lyndon B Johnson.
- General Douglas MacArthur.
- Ho Chi Minh.
- Richard Nixon.
- Kim II-Sung.
- Harry Truman.

Key Events
Some of the key events and developments you will study on this course include:

- The origins of the Cold War.
- The invasion of South Korea.
- The stalemate in the Korean War.
- The first Indo-China war.
- The civil war in South Vietnam.
- The Gulf of Tonkin incident.
- Operation Rolling Thunder.
- The Tet Offensive.
- The My Lai Massacre.
- Events at the Kent State University.
- The USA withdrawal from Vietnam.

Assessment
The Conflict and Tension in Asia, 1950 - 1975 course is part of paper 1 (2 hours). You should spend 1 hour on this section of the paper. There will be 4 exam questions which will assess what you have learned from the course.

- Question 1 is worth 4 marks. It requires you to examine a source and explain its meaning in its historical context.
- Question 2 is worth 12 marks. It requires you to examine 2 sources and assesses your ability to evaluate sources for a particular purpose.
- Question 3 is worth 8 marks. It requires to you to explain and analyse historical events in relation to cause and consequence.

Question 4 is worth 16 marks, plus 4 marks for spelling, punctuation and grammar. You are required to make judgement about the importance of an event or development in an extended response.

Revision! A dreaded word. Everyone knows it's coming, everyone knows how much it helps with your exam performance, and everyone struggles to get started! We know you want to do the best you can in your GCSEs, but schools aren't always clear on the best way to revise. This can leave students wondering:

- ✓ How should I plan my revision time?
- ✓ How can I beat procrastination?
- ✓ What methods should I use? Flash cards? Re-reading my notes? Highlighting?

Luckily, you no longer need to guess at the answers. Education researchers have looked at all the available revision studies, and the jury is in. They've come up with some key pointers on the best ways to revise, as well as some thoughts on popular revision methods that aren't so helpful. The next few pages will help you understand what we know about the best revision methods.

How can I beat procrastination?

This is an age-old question, and it applies to adults as well! Have a look at our top three tips below.

◎ Reward yourself

When we think a task we have to do is going to be boring, hard or uncomfortable, we often put if off and do something more 'fun' instead. But we often don't really enjoy the 'fun' activity because we feel guilty about avoiding what we should be doing. Instead, get your work done and promise yourself a reward after you complete it. Whatever treat you choose will seem all the sweeter, and you'll feel proud for doing something you found difficult. Just do it!

◎ Just do it!

We tend to procrastinate when we think the task we have to do is going to be difficult or dull. The funny thing is, the most uncomfortable part is usually making ourselves sit down and start it in the first place. Once you begin, it's usually not nearly as bad as you anticipated.

◎ Pomodoro technique

The pomodoro technique helps you trick your brain by telling it you only have to focus for a short time. Set a timer for 20 minutes and focus that whole period on your revision. Turn off your phone, clear your desk, and work. At the end of the 20 minutes, you get to take a break for five. Then, do another 20 minutes. You'll usually find your rhythm and it becomes easier to carry on because it's only for a short, defined chunk of time.

Spaced practice

We tend to arrange our revision into big blocks. For example, you might tell yourself: "This week I'll do all my revision for the Cold War, then next week I'll do the Medicine Through Time unit."

This is called **massed practice**, because all revision for a single topic is done as one big mass.

But there's a better way! Try **spaced practice** instead. Instead of putting all revision sessions for one topic into a sin block, space them out. See the example below for how it works.

This means planning ahead, rather than leaving revision to the last minute - but the evidence strongly suggests it's worth it. You'll remember much more from your revision if you use **spaced practice** rather than organising it into b blocks. Whichever method you choose, though, remember to reward yourself with breaks.

Spaced practice (more effective):

week 1	week 2	week 3	week 4
Topic 1	Topic 1	Topic 1	Topic 1
Topic 2	Topic 2	Topic 2	Topic 2
Topic 3	Topic 3	Topic 3	Topic 3
Topic 4	Topic 4	Topic 4	Topic 4

Massed practice (less effective)

week 1	week 2	week 3	week 4
Topic 1	Topic 2	Topic 3	Topic 4

Quizzes, amazing exam preparation tools and more at GCSEHistory.com

What methods should I use to revise?

Self-testing/flash cards

Self explanation/mind-mapping

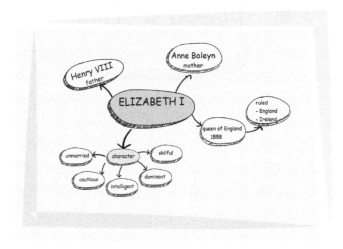

The research shows a clear winner for revision methods - **self-testing**. A good way to do this is with **flash cards**. Flash cards are really useful for helping you recall short – but important – pieces of information, like names and dates.

Side A - question

Side B - answer

Write questions on one side of the cards, and the answers on the back. This makes answering the questions and then testing yourself easy. Put all the cards you get right in a pile to one side, and only repeat the test with the ones you got wrong - this will force you to work on your weaker areas.

pile with right answers

pile with wrong answers

As this book has a quiz question structure itself, you can use it for this technique.

Another good revision method is **self-explanation**. This is where you explain how and why one piece of information from your course linked with another piece.

This can be done with **mind-maps**, where you draw the links and then write explanations for how they connect. For example, President Truman is connected with anti-communism because of the Truman Doctrine.

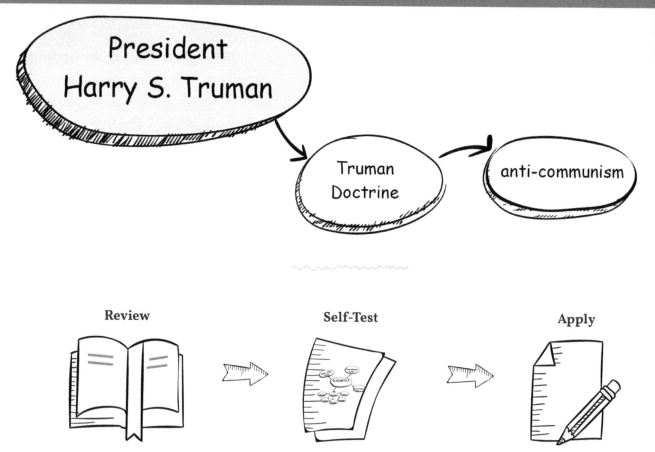

Review

Self-Test

Apply

Start by highlighting or re-reading to create your flashcards for self-testing.

Test yourself with flash cards. Make mind maps to explain the concepts.

Apply your knowledge on pract exam questions.

Which revision techniques should I be cautious about?

Highlighting and **re-reading** are not necessarily bad strategies - but the research does say they're less effective th flash cards and mind-maps.

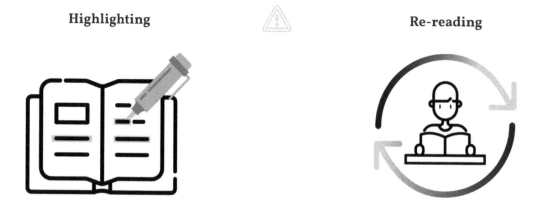

Highlighting

Re-reading

If you do use these methods, make sure they are **the first step to creating flash cards**. Really engage with the mat as you go, rather than switching to autopilot.

TIMELINE

1945

August - Korea is divided into 2 nations along the 38th parallel *(p.27)*

1946

December - Beginning of the 1st Indochina war against the Vietminh and the Imperial French powers in Vietnam *(p.47)*

1947

ch - President Harry Truman announces the policy of containment, ch became known as the Truman Doctrine *(p.20)*

1949

The Cold War begins *(p.16)*

1949 - A communist government comes to power in China and the People's Republic of China is established *(p.28)*

1950

June - Kim Il-Sung launches an invasion of South Korea *(p.31)*

- President Truman sends $15 million in aid to France to fight the minh, marking the beginning of US involvement in Vietnam *(p.48)*

tember - UN forces led by General Douglas MacArthur arrive in th Korea *(p.34)*

ober - UN forces advance beyond the 38th parallel into North ea *(p.36)*

ober - China enters the Korean war to support Kim Il-Sung's forces *7)*

1952

November - Dwight D Eisenhower is elected President of the United States and promises to end the stalemate in Korea *(p.101)*

1953

- Peace settlement agreed, marking the end of the Korean War 40)

1954

April - Dwight D Eisenhower first articulates the concept of the 'Domino Theory' *(p.50)*

May - France surrenders to the Vietminh after defeat at the battle of Dien Bien Phu *(p.51)*

July - The Geneva Accords divides Vietnam at the 17th parallel into North Vietnam and South Vietnam *(p.52)*

1955

uary - Dwight D Eisenhower sends the first shipment of military aid South Vietnam *(p.49)*

1957

July - Civil war breaks out in South Vietnam in opposition to Ngo Dinh Diem's government *(p.56)*

1960

vember - John F Kennedy elected President of the United States 103)*

December - The Vietcong is formed *(p.58)*

1962

January - There are now 11,000 US military advisors in Vietnam *(p.57)*

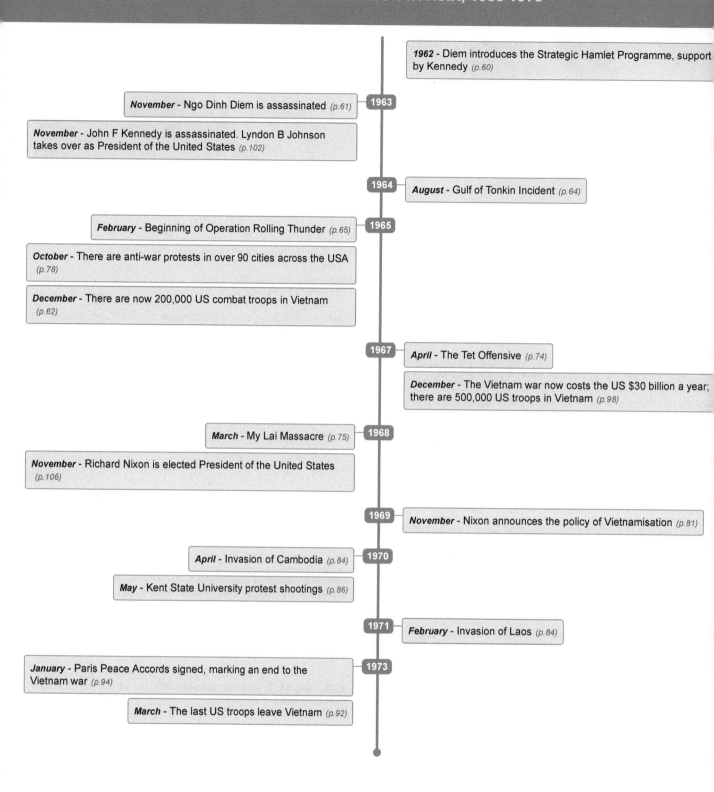

1962 - Diem introduces the Strategic Hamlet Programme, support by Kennedy *(p.60)*

1963

November - Ngo Dinh Diem is assassinated *(p.61)*

November - John F Kennedy is assassinated. Lyndon B Johnson takes over as President of the United States *(p.102)*

1964

August - Gulf of Tonkin Incident *(p.64)*

1965

February - Beginning of Operation Rolling Thunder *(p.65)*

October - There are anti-war protests in over 90 cities across the USA *(p.78)*

December - There are now 200,000 US combat troops in Vietnam *(p.62)*

1967

April - The Tet Offensive *(p.74)*

December - The Vietnam war now costs the US $30 billion a year; there are 500,000 US troops in Vietnam *(p.98)*

1968

March - My Lai Massacre *(p.75)*

November - Richard Nixon is elected President of the United States *(p.106)*

1969

November - Nixon announces the policy of Vietnamisation *(p.81)*

1970

April - Invasion of Cambodia *(p.84)*

May - Kent State University protest shootings *(p.86)*

1971

February - Invasion of Laos *(p.84)*

1973

January - Paris Peace Accords signed, marking an end to the Vietnam war *(p.94)*

March - The last US troops leave Vietnam *(p.92)*

THE COLD WAR

'Although the shooting war is over, we are in the midst of a cold war which is getting warmer.'
Bernard Baruch, 1947

What was the Cold War?

The Cold War was a state of hostility that existed between the USSR and the USA in the second half of the 20th cent

What is the definition of a cold war?

A cold war is a conflict in which there is no direct fighting between the two sides. It is fought through economic and political actions.

When was the Cold War?

The Cold War lasted from 1945 to 1991.

Who was involved in the Cold War?

The Cold War was between the USA and its allies, and the Soviet Union, its satellite states and its allies.

What were the long-term causes of the Cold War?

There are 7 main reasons the Cold War happened:

- ☑ In October 1917, the Bolsheviks seized power in Russia. By 1921 they had created the first communist state. They anti-capitalism and wanted to spread the communist revolution across the world.
- ☑ America and Britain did not trust the USSR as Russia had withdrawn from the First World War in 1917, despite b a member of the Triple Entente with Britain and France.
- ☑ The USSR did not trust the USA, France and Britain because they sent troops to fight against the Bolsheviks in th Russian Civil War.
- ☑ In the 1920s, the USA suffered from the First Red Scare and was hostile towards the USSR.
- ☑ The USSR was angry it was not recognised as a country by the USA until 1933.
- ☑ The relationship between the USSR and the West deteriorated before the Second World War. The Soviet Union w angry at not being invited to the Munich Conference in 1938.
- ☑ When the USSR signed the Nazi-Soviet Pact in 1939, Britain and France were horrified.

How was the Cold War fought?

The Cold War was fought in 7 key ways:

- ☑ Propaganda.
- ☑ Spying or espionage, such as using spy planes to take photographs.
- ☑ An arms race to have the most developed weapons, particularly nuclear missiles.
- ☑ A space race competing for success in space, such as being the first nation to put a man on the moon.
- ☑ Financial aid or loans to other countries to gain their support.
- ☑ Proxy wars, where the USA and the USSR became involved in conflicts in other countries. An example is the Kor War *(p.22)* of 1950-53.
- ☑ Threats made by either side.

What created tension between the Soviet Union and the USA at the beginning of the Cold War?

The ideological differences between the superpowers created tension between them. The Soviet Union supported communism, whereas the USA and Britain were capitalist countries.

What were the different ideologies in the Cold War?

The Cold War was a result of ideological differences between the two sides:

- ✅ The USSR was communist. Communism is a system where there is no private ownership of land, property or business. The aim is to achieve economic equality for the benefit of the people through central control of the state economy.
- ✅ The USA was capitalist. Capitalism is a system where individuals are free to own land, property and businesses to create wealth and accept there will be economic inequality as a result.

Why were the USA and the USSR considered superpowers during the Cold War?

The USSR and the USA were considered to be superpowers because they possessed 3 key things:

- ✅ Massive military might, including nuclear weapons.
- ✅ Economic might.
- ✅ The ability to dominate other countries.

Why was Stalin distrustful of Truman at the beginning at the Cold War?

Joseph Stalin was distrustful of Harry S Truman for 3 key reasons:

- ✅ Truman was anti-communist.
- ✅ He tried to control the Potsdam meeting.
- ✅ He successfully tested the atomic bomb without consulting Stalin and used it in the Hiroshima and Nagasaki bombings in the days after Potsdam.

Why did Britain ally closely with the USA at the beginning at the Cold War?

Britain was concerned about communism spreading. The nation's economy was severely impacted after the Second World War so it couldn't act against the Soviet Union alone.

DID YOU KNOW?

The first known mention of the term 'Cold War' was made by English author George Orwell in a 1945 essay titled, 'You and the Atomic Bomb'.

THE CAUSES OF THE COLD WAR

'There are at the present time two great nations in the world...the Russians and the Americans...
Their starting point is different and their courses are not the same, yet each of them seems marked
out by the will of Heaven to sway the destinies of half the globe.'
Historian Alexis de Tocqueville, 1831

Who caused the Cold War?

Historians debate whether the USA or USSR bore greater responsibility for the outbreak of the Cold War *(p. 16)*.

How did the USA cause the Cold War?

Some historians argue the USA was mainly responsible for the start of the Cold War *(p. 16)* for 6 key reasons:

- ✅ The Marshall Plan, the Truman Doctrine *(p. 19)*, the policy of containment and the creation of NATO were seen as aggressive moves.

- ✅ President Truman was openly anti-communist, which caused greater tension. His relationship with Stalin was worse than that of Roosevelt, his predecessor.
- ✅ The USA didn't inform the Soviets about their work on developing the atom bomb. The Soviets found out through their spies and felt betrayed.
- ✅ Stalin was not consulted over the formation of Trizonia or the adoption of the Deutschmark, despite agreement t decisions over Germany would be made jointly.
- ✅ Stalin saw the USA's refusal to leave West Berlin as a threat.
- ✅ Both sides participated in the nuclear arms race.

How did the USSR cause the Cold War?

Some historians argue the USSR was mainly responsible for causing the Cold War *(p.16)* for 6 key reasons:

- ✅ Stalin went against some of the promises he made at Yalta, such as occupying Poland and refusing to allow easter European countries to have free elections.
- ✅ Instead of free elections in eastern Europe, Stalin ensured communist puppet governments - which he could cont - gained power. This happened in Czechoslovakia, Poland, Hungary, Romania, Bulgaria and East Germany. This v seen as a threat to capitalism.
- ✅ The Red Army's occupation of eastern Europe was seen as a threat, and an attempt to control the whole of Europe
- ✅ Comecon, Cominform and the Warsaw Pact were seen as aggressive moves.
- ✅ The Berlin Blockade was an extremely aggressive act.
- ✅ Both sides participated in the nuclear arms race.

DID YOU KNOW?

Soviet archives about the Cold War were opened in 1991. This had a huge impact on historical interpretations of the conflict.

THE DIFFERENCES BETWEEN CAPITALISM AND COMMUNISI

'The inherent vice of capitalism is the unequal sharing of blessings; the inherent virtue of communism
is the equal sharing of miseries.'
Winston Churchill

What is the difference between capitalism and communism?

Capitalism and communism are two different ideologies, with opposing ideas about how to run and organise a count

What are the differences between capitalist and communist ideas about how to run and organise a country?

Capitalist and communist countries have differing ideas on many subjects, including: how businesses should be run; voting systems that decide who rules a nation; organisation of the economy; distribution of wealth.

What are the differences between capitalist and communist ideas about how businesses should be run?

A capitalist country believes businesses should be owned by private individuals, with no government interference, ar allowed to make money for themselves. By contrast, communists believe the government should own all businesses.

What are the differences between capitalist and communist ideas about voting systems?

A capitalist country believes there should be democratic elections, with a choice of 2 or more parties to vote for, when deciding who runs the country. By contrast, a communist country believes in a one-party government, with no voting or choice in who runs the country.

What are the differences between capitalist and communist ideas about how the economy should be run?

A capitalist country believes in a free economy, with businesses in competition with each other. By contrast, a communist country believes in strict controls on the economy, so that everything is run by the state, for the state.

What are the differences between capitalist and communist ideas about the distribution of wealth?

In a capitalist country there are great differences in wealth between groups of people. By contrast, a communist country believes wealth should be shared equally among the people.

What was significant about the differences between capitalist and communist ideas about how a country should be run and organised?

Having different ideas about how a country should be run and organised does not always mean nations have to become enemies. However. this difference in ideas was significant for 4 key reasons:

- ☑ It resulted in the ideological conflict between the USA and the USSR that defined the Cold War *(p.16)* between 1945 and 1990.
- ☑ Both the USA and USSR thought their system was the way in which all countries should be organised and run.
- ☑ The USA believed the USSR was intent on spreading communism, so it was seen as threat to the American way of life.
- ☑ The USSR felt the actions of capitalist countries from 1917 to 1945 were aggressive, and that its way of life was under threat.

DID YOU KNOW?

Americans felt their way of life was under threat from communism in the 1920s, resulting in a period of hysteria called the 'Red Scare'.

THE TRUMAN DOCTRINE

'The seeds of totalitarian regimes are nurtured by misery and want. They spread and grow in the evil soil of poverty and strife.'
President Harry Truman, 1947

What was the Truman Doctrine?

The Truman Doctrine was an American policy which was anti-communist and involved the containment of communism. It led to the Marshall Plan.

When did the Truman Doctrine begin?

President Harry S Truman announced his doctrine on 12th March, 1947.

Why was the Truman Doctrine established?

There were 3 main reasons the Truman Doctrine was created:

- ☑ Britain could not afford to give any more military support to the Greek government in the civil war against Gree communists.
- ☑ The USA promised $400 million in aid to Greece and Turkey to help win the war against the Greek communists
- ☑ It aimed to contain the spread of communism by giving military and economic assistance to any country threate by communism.

What were the main points of the Truman Doctrine?

The Truman Doctrine contained 3 key points:

- ☑ It stated the world had a choice between communism, or capitalism and democracy;
- ☑ The USA would send troops and economic aid to countries threatened by communism so it was contained and c not spread;
- ☑ The USA would no longer follow an isolationist foreign policy and would now get involved in the affairs of other countries, rather than stay out of them.

What conditions were there in order for countries to receive aid under the Truman Doctrine?

Countries had to choose capitalism over communism in order to receive aid from the USA.

What was the importance of the Truman Doctrine?

There were 4 main reasons the Truman Doctrine was important:

- ☑ It meant the USA officially abandoned its isolationist foreign policy and would play an active role in the world.
- ☑ It meant the USA was on a potential collision course with the USSR as the doctrine was directed against the spre communism.
- ☑ It directly resulted in the creation of the Marshall Plan.
- ☑ It resulted in the further deterioration in the relationship between the USA and the USSR.

DID YOU KNOW?

The Truman Doctrine was, in fact, the declaration of the Cold War.

THE POLICY OF CONTAINMENT

The containment of communism became a key aim of American foreign policy from the 1940s onwards.

What was containment?

Containment was America's policy on communism. It involved preventing it from spreading to new countries, rathe than attacking existing communist nations.

When was containment introduced?

Containment was first introduced in 1947.

What policy introduced the idea of containment?

Containment was first set out in the Truman Doctrine *(p. 19)* and the Marshall Plan.

What methods of containment were used?

The USA used 4 main methods of containment:

- ☑ It aimed to build bigger and better weapons faster than the USSR. This led to both sides becoming embroiled in an arms race.
- ☑ It offered economic support for countries threatened by communism.
- ☑ It forged alliances with other countries.
- ☑ It gave military assistance to countries threatened by communism.

Why was containment needed?

After the Second World War, the apparent need for containment was reinforced by 4 main global events:

- ☑ In 1947-48, eastern European countries were taken over by communist governments.
- ☑ In 1948, North Korea became communist.
- ☑ In August 1949, the USSR successfully tested an atomic bomb.
- ☑ China became a communist country in 1949.

What alliances were formed as part of containment?

The USA formed 4 main alliances in response to the threat of communism:

- ☑ The most important was the North Atlantic Treaty Organisation, or NATO, formed in 1949.
- ☑ The South-East Asia Treaty Organisation (SEATO) was formed in September 1954 between the USA, New Zealand, Australia, the Philippines, Thailand, Pakistan, Britain and France.
- ☑ CENTO, or the Central Treaty Organisation, was formed in February 1955 between Iran, Iraq, Pakistan, Turkey and the UK.
- ☑ The USSR responded by setting up the Warsaw Pact in May 1955. The USSR, Romania, Bulgaria, Czechoslovakia, East Germany, Albania, Poland and Hungary were members.

How was military assistance used as part of containment?

The USA was prepared to provide weapons, military advice, training, troops, technical support and personnel to countries threatened by communism.

When was military assistance used as part of containment?

Examples of 3 significant occasions when the USA provided military support for countries threatened by communism were:

- ☑ 1950 - 1953 - in Korea, with UN support.
- ☑ 1961 - The Bay of Pigs invasion in Cuba.
- ☑ 1955 - 1975 - Vietnam.

DID YOU KNOW?

The first test of the policy of containment came in Greece and Turkey.

THE KOREAN WAR

The Korean War was a major escalation of Cold War tensions, and only narrowly avoided the deployment of nuclear weapons.

What was the Korean War?

The Korean War was fought between North and South Korea and was the first flashpoint of the Cold War in Asia.

Where did the Korean War take place?

In Korea, which is between China to the west and Japan to the east.

When was the Korean War?

The Korean War began in June 1950 and finished in 1954.

What were the key phases of the Korean War?

There were 5 main phases to the war, including:

- [x] North Korea invaded South Korea on 25th June, 1950.
- [x] A UN army, made up mostly of American military and led by General Douglas MacArthur *(p.104)*, arrived in Korea September 1950 to push back against the North Korean invasion *(p.31)*.
- [x] In October 1950, UN forces advanced into North Korean territory.
- [x] On 25th October, China entered the war. Together with the North Korean army, they pushed the UN forces back below the 38th parallel. This resulted in a stalemate for over two years.
- [x] After peace talks on 27th July, 1953, the UN, China and North Korea signed a peace treaty.

What were the long-term causes that led to the Korean War?

Several important long-term events led to the Korean War, including:

- [x] The history of Korea was shaped by many wars over who would control it. Both China and Japan ruled the nation significant periods of time.
- [x] Between 1910 and 1945, Korea was controlled by Japan. This changed at the end of the Second World War.
- [x] At the end of the Second World War, the Japanese in the north surrendered to the USSR, and those in the south to USA.

At the end of the Second World War, what was the situation that led to the Korean War?

At the end of the Second World War, when Japan surrendered and Korea was occupied by Soviet troops in the north American troops in the south, the following happened:

- [x] The country was divided into two separate zones along the 38th parallel, a circle of latitude that runs across the middle of Korea.
- [x] The division of Korea *(p.27)* was supposed to be temporary. The aim was for it to be a united and independent coun The United Nations *(p.25)* was to organise elections that would achieve this.
- [x] Instead of free elections, the Soviets in North Korea enabled Korean communist Kim Il-Sung *(p.107)* to take contro the nation without being elected.
- [x] There was an election in US-controlled South Korea, and USA supporter and capitalist figure Syngman Rhee *(p.10* became its leader.
- [x] At this point, North and South Korea became two different nations. The USSR zone in the north became the Peopl Republic of Korea, and the US zone in the south became the Republic of Korea.
- [x] While the leaders in both North and South Korea were nationalists and wanted a united country after the war, the wanted the nation to be led by different ideologies - capitalism in the south and communism in the north.

What were the key events in the build-up to the Korean War?

The leaders of North and South Korea each saw themselves as the legitimate and rightful ruler of the whole nation. Events in the build-up to the Korean War included:

- ☑ Due to the attitude of superiority from both sides there were a number of clashes on the border between North and South Korea.
- ☑ Kim Il-Sung *(p.107)*, the leader of North Korea, visited Stalin in 1949 to ask for his support in an invasion of South Korea. He felt this would be welcome in the south as an effort to reunite the two nations.
- ☑ Stalin did not think it was the right time as he did not want a fight against US troops still stationed in South Korea.
- ☑ In 1950, Stalin's circumstances had changed. The US troops had left South Korea; communists were in power in China; and the USSR had its own nuclear weapons and had cracked the secret codes used by the USA to talk to other nations. As a result, Stalin felt any future actions in Korea would not meet American opposition.
- ☑ Stalin began sending tanks, artillery and aircraft to North Korea and gave the go-ahead for an invasion of the south.
- ☑ Stalin stated USSR soldiers would not be directly involved, and if further supplies were needed North Korea should ask China.

What started the Korean War?

The Korean War broke out when North Korea invaded South Korea on 25th June, 1950.

Why did the UN get involved in the Korean War?

When the south was invaded, the USA brought the matter to the UN which passed a resolution calling for North Korea to withdraw. When it did not, the UN sent international troops - mostly American - to force it out. In this way the USA could argue it was acting against international aggression rather than following its containment policy *(p.20)*.

Why did America get involved in the Korean War?

There were 3 key reasons America got involved in the Korean War:

- ☑ President Truman was concerned communism was spreading in Asia.
- ☑ China's fall to communism in 1949 heightened this fear.
- ☑ Truman was also concerned about Stalin's use of Cominform to encourage countries to turn to communism.

What was America's role in the Korean War?

America had 2 main roles in the Korean War:

- ☑ United Nations *(p.25)* troops, mainly American and led by US General Douglas MacArthur *(p.104)*, were sent to Korea. The North was supported by the Soviet Union.
- ☑ UN forces were able to push North Korea back to the Chinese border, but in late 1950 China joined the war and the UN had to retreat.

What ended the Korean War?

After three years of fighting an armistice was agreed, which re-established the border between North and South Korea.

What effect did the Korean War have on America?

There were 5 main consequences of the Korean War:

- ☑ It demonstrated the USA's commitment to containing communism and led to a tripling of military spending to prevent its spread.
- ☑ To stop the spread of communism in Asia, the Southeast Asia Treaty Organisation (SEATO) was set up in September 1954. Britain, Pakistan, USA, Thailand, France, Australia, the Philippines and New Zealand all joined.
- ☑ The sacking of General MacArthur over his proposal to deploy nuclear bombs against North Korea underlined the USA's caution with regard to using nuclear weapons.

- ✅ The Soviet Union doubled the size of the Red Army, from 2.8 million in 1950 to 5.6 million in 1955.
- ✅ As the war did not escalate further, it showed neither superpower was prepared to engage in direct military confrontation with the other, preferring instead to fight proxy wars.

Who were the winners and losers of the Korean War?

Given the cost to human life, and that the Korean War was a 'war within a war', it is difficult to assign victory to one or the other. North Korea, South Korea, the USA, the United Nations (p.25), the USSR and China all experienced gains losses, and were therefore both winners and losers.

How could Korea be seen as a winner in the Korean War?

Historians see neither South Korea nor North Korea as a winner of the conflict; the two nations remain divided to t] day.

How could the USA be seen as a winner in the Korean War?

The USA can be seen as a winner as it successfully contained communism and stopped it spreading throughout Asi: Truman Doctrine (p.19) was a success.

How could the United Nations be seen as a winner in the Korean War?

The UN's predecessor, the League of Nations, had crumbled in its efforts to stop aggression before the Second World War. The UN's actions in Korea proved this kind of organisation could successfully halt conflict in the world. Its accomplishments gained it great respect.

How could the USSR be seen as a winner in the Korean War?

As a result of the Korean War, the USSR developed a closer alliance with communist China.

How could China be seen as a winner in the Korean War?

The Korean War brought China a reputation as one of the world's leading military powers and enabled it to develop closer alliance with the USSR.

How could Korea be seen as a loser in the Korean War?

Korea can be seen as a loser in the war for a number of reasons:

- ✅ There was a huge human cost - more than 800,000 North and South Korean civilians lost their lives.
- ✅ Approximately 80 per cent of both North and South Korea's industrial buildings were destroyed.
- ✅ Much of Korea's housing and transportation infrastructure was bombed.
- ✅ There was a desperate housing shortage in North Korea. Many people had no option but to live in caves.

How could the USA be seen as a loser in the Korean War?

The USA could be seen as a loser for a number of reasons:

- ✅ It was responsible for the huge loss of civilian life in Korea and had used weapons such as napalm, which damage reputation.
- ✅ It had increase military spending by a huge amount in order to fight the war.
- ✅ It failed to defeat communism in North Korea.
- ✅ The Korean War cost the USA its relations with China.

How could the United Nations be seen as a loser in the Korean War?

Due to the USA's significant involvement in the war, some people started to question if the United Nations (p.25) was 'puppet' controlled by America. In some ways, therefore, the war damaged its reputation.

Quizzes, amazing exam preparation tools and more at GCSEHistory.com

How could the USSR be seen as a loser in the Korean War?

The war led to increased tensions with the USA, the Soviet Union's rival in the Cold War *(p.16)*. It also led to a weapons build-up, with both nations entering the arms race. This became a huge economic burden to the USSR.

How could China be seen as a loser in the Korean War?

China was poor compared to the other world powers, and the war proved a huge economic burden. It failed to help North Korea unite the 2 nations under communism, and its involvement led to the USA cutting off all trade and political links with China for 25 years.

DID YOU KNOW?

The Korean War, with approximately 3 million fatalities, was the first time the Cold War turned 'hot' and broke out into violence.

THE UNITED NATIONS

'More than ever before in human history, we share a common destiny. We can master it only if we face it together. And that, my friends, is why we have the United Nations.'
UN Secretary General Kofi Annan, speaking in 1999

What was the United Nations?

The United Nations was - and continues to be - a world organisation committed to establishing international peace and security. It works to develop friendly relations among countries, achieve international cooperation, and acts as a body to resolve issues of conflict.

When was the United Nations created?

The United Nations was created in 1945, at the end of the Second World War.

Where is the headquarters of the United Nations?

The headquarters of the United Nations is in New York City, USA.

Who was involved with the United Nations?

The United Nations today has 193 members. However, when it was first created in 1945, there were 51 members including:

- ✅ From Europe: the UK and France.
- ✅ From the Americas: the USA and Canada, Mexico, and Brazil.
- ✅ From Asia: the USSR and China.
- ✅ From Oceania: Australia and New Zealand.

Why was the United Nations created?

The United Nations was created in order to create a peaceful and more harmonious world in the aftermath of the Second World War.

What were the United Nations main principles?

The United Nations was created with a set of core principles:

- ☑ To keep world peace and security.
- ☑ To bring nations closer together.
- ☑ To help nations solve international disputes.
- ☑ To help nations cooperate to meet common goals.

What is the role of the United Nations?

The United Nations has 3 main roles:

- ☑ It provides countries with a place to discuss problems and give their views on world issues.
- ☑ It holds meetings called the 'General Assembly', which is its main forum for debate.
- ☑ It takes action on certain international issues set out in the UN Charter.

What was the role of the United Nations' Security Council?

The Security Council made all the important decisions that impacted world peace and security. It worked in 2 main ways:

- ☑ It had 15 members, 5 of which - Great Britain, France, USA, China and the USSR - were permanent. The remaining were non-permanent and attended meetings on a rotation.
- ☑ For a decision to be made, 9 countries - including all 5 permanent members - had to agree. This meant permanent members could veto decisions.

How did the Cold War impact the United Nations?

The Cold War *(p.16)* impacted the United Nations in 3 key ways:

- ☑ During the Korean War *(p.22)*, the USA and the USSR often squabbled with each other in meetings. Decision-making was difficult as they would often use their veto to block suggestions.
- ☑ China was a founding member of the United Nations. However, when it became a communist country, the Security Council had to agree to the new communist nation being allowed to join. This caused further conflict between the USA and USSR.
- ☑ When the USA chose to recognise Chiang Kai-shek, the non-communist nationalist leader, as the rightful leader of China, the USSR left the meeting in which China's membership was decided.

DID YOU KNOW?

The UN was founded after the Second World War to replace the League of Nations, which had been ineffective in preventing the conflict.

THE DIVISION OF KOREA

*'In a meeting in August 1945, a colonel and I late at night studied a map of the Korean peninsula.
Working under great pressure, we had a formidable task: to pick a zone for the American occupation.
We looked just north of Seoul for a convenient dividing line but couldn't find a natural geographic
line. We saw the 38th parallel and decided to recommend that.'*
Dean Rusk, US Secretary of State, 1961-1969

What was the division of Korea?

The division of Korea was the separation of the country into two nations at the end of the Second World War.

When was Korea divided?

The division of Korea took place between 10th - 17th August, 1945.

How was Korea divided?

Korea was divided into two separate zones - North Korea and South Korea - along the 38th parallel. This line divided the country almost exactly in half.

Why was Korea divided?

Korea was divided after the break up of the Japanese Empire. Japan had controlled the country since the beginning of the 20th century, until its defeat at the end of the Second World War. Japanese soldiers in the north had surrendered to Soviet troops, and soldiers in the south had surrendered to the US.

What happened to the north when Korea was divided?

In the north, Stalin appointed Kim Il-Sung *(p.107)*, a communist who had trained in the USSR, as leader. No elections were held, even though it had been agreed when the country was first divided that they would take place. The country became known as the People's Republic of Korea, or North Korea.

What happened to the south when Korea was divided?

Elections were held in the US-controlled southern zone, in keeping with the agreement. The new president was Syngman Rhee *(p.107)*, a capitalist with close ties to America. The country became known as the Republic of Korea, or South Korea.

What was the impact of the division of Korea?

The division of Korea had 3 important impacts:

- ☑ The division of Korea led to further tensions in the Cold War *(p.16)* between the USA and the USSR.
- ☑ Tensions between the communist North and capitalist-backed South escalated into conflict from 1950 to 1953.
- ☑ The country remains divided to the present day, even though the division was supposed to be temporary.

DID YOU KNOW?

Some historians argue the decision to divide Korea was a measure to prevent Soviet forces from occupying the whole country.

NATIONALISM IN KOREA

'My God is none other than the people. Only the popular masses are omniscient and omnipotent and almighty on earth. Therefore, my lifetime motto is: The people are my God.'
Kim Il-Sung

What role did nationalism play in the outbreak of the Korean War?

Nationalism played a significant role in the Korean War *(p.22)*, shaping the actions of the leaders in both North and South Korea.

Why did nationalism play a role in the outbreak of the Korean War?

The leaders of both North and South Korea, Kim Il-sung *(p.107)* and Syngman Rhee *(p.107)*, were strong nationalists committed to the reunification of Korea after the Second World War.

Why did nationalism create problems leading to the outbreak of the Korean War?

Nationalism created a problem because, while both leaders wanted to see Korea reunified, they each believed the country should follow a different set of ideologies.

DID YOU KNOW?

Both North and South Korean people were very proud of being Korean, and were committed to reunification.

US RELATIONS WITH CHINA

US relations with China helped determine the course of events in Korea.

What were US relations with China like in 1950?

At the time of the outbreak of the Korean War *(p.22)* in 1950, US relations with China were hostile.

Why were US relations with China in 1950 hostile?

US relations with China were hostile for 3 key reasons:

- ☑ The US had previously backed the anti-communist Chiang Kai-shek in the Chinese civil war. The communists w the war and took over the government.
- ☑ This scared America, who was committed to containing communism and was convinced it would now spread throughout Asia.
- ☑ US spies suggested the USSR and China were trying to support communist takeovers in other areas of Asia, inclu Indonesia, Burma, the Philippines, and Korea.

What was significant about US relations with China in 1950?

US relations with China were significant for the following reasons:

- ☑ The hostility between them is considered a key cause of the Korean War *(p.22)*. It certainly shaped America's actio when North Korea launched its invasion of the south.
- ☑ Their relationship shaped the direction of US policy in Vietnam, spanning 5 presidents. Each one further commit the USA to the region as he did not want to be the leader who lost Vietnam to communism, as Truman did with China.

Quizzes, amazing exam preparation tools and more at GCSEHistory.com

THE CAUSES OF THE KOREAN WAR

'Eventually the Korean War will be understood as one of the most destructive and one of the most important wars of the 20th century.'
Bruce Cumings, American historian

What caused the Korean War?

The Korean War *(p.22)* originated from internal conflicts between the communist north and the non-communist south. There were also external factors relating to the Cold War *(p.16)* and the development of communism in China.

What key reasons caused the Korean War?

There were 6 key causes of the Korean War *(p.22)*:

- ☑ The Cold War *(p.16)*.
- ☑ The US policy of containment.
- ☑ The division of Korea *(p.27)*.
- ☑ Different governments in Korea.
- ☑ The development of communism in China.
- ☑ Interference from other countries.

How did the Cold War cause the Korean War?

The Korean War *(p.22)* was born out of the ideological conflict of the Cold War *(p.16)* that developed over a number of years. It caused the Korean War in the a number of ways including:

- ☑ The Korean War *(p.22)* was a proxy of the Cold War *(p.16)*. The world's two leading superpowers - the USA and the USSR - were in an ideological conflict, competing for dominance. However, they could only fight through proxy wars due to the threat of nuclear warfare.
- ☑ When communist North Korea invaded South Korea, the USA was able to fight communist Russia without direct confrontation. The Korean War *(p.22)* was an extension of the Cold War *(p.16)*.
- ☑ The Cold War *(p.16)* rivalry between the USSR and the USA was a critical cause of the Korean War *(p.22)*, as North Korea would not invade South Korea without Stalin's permission. He gave it as it strengthened his position in the context of the Cold War.

How did the policy of containment cause the Korean War?

The policy of containment was a short-term cause of the Korean War *(p.22)* and contributed in 4 key ways:

- ☑ In 1947 the President of the USA, Harry S Truman, committed to helping any country under threat from a communist takeover. This was known as the Truman Doctrine *(p.19)* and meant that, when North Korea invaded South Korea, America helped the south.
- ☑ Until 1950, most of the USA's efforts in fighting the spread of communism were focused on Europe. However, in 1949, the communists came to power in China, despite America's efforts to support the anti-communist government.
- ☑ Truman and the US government believed communism would spread throughout Asia. The USA was worried the fall of China would lead to other neighbouring countries following suit - South Korea, and then Japan.

☑ Stalin's support of the invasion did not bring about the war alone. The USA was determined to prevent any more nations in Asia falling to communism.

How did the division of Korea cause the Korean War?

There were 2 key reasons the division caused the Korean War (p.22):

☑ The division of Korea (p.27) along the 38th parallel was supposed to be temporary. North and South Korea both wanted to unite, but had different ideas about the style of government. The North wanted a united communist nation, while the South wanted a united capitalist nation.

☑ The division of Korea (p.27), and the different styles of government, meant the USA and the USSR were both committed to supporting an opposing side. It was, therefore, an extension of the Cold War (p.16).

How did the different governments in North and South Korea cause the Korean War?

North and South Korea were each ruled by a separate government with with different ideas. However, both were committed to uniting Korea. This triggered the Korean War (p.22) for a number of reasons:

☑ North Korea was controlled by the communist Kim II-Sung (p.107), who had strong links to the USSR.

☑ Kim II-Sung (p.107) was committed to uniting Korea as a communist nation.

☑ Kim II-Sung (p.107) persuaded Stalin, leader of the USSR, and Mao Zedong, ruler of China, to back an invasion of South Korea. Stalin saw this as an opportunity to continue the Cold War (p.16) through proxy.

☑ South Korea was controlled by anti-communist Syngman Rhee (p.107), who had boasted about planning an attack take over the north and unite Korea as a capitalist nation. This was the excuse Kim II-Sung (p.107) needed to invad

How did the interference from other countries cause the Korean War?

The support (and interference) of other countries helped trigger the Korean War (p.22), because neither North nor Sou could have fought without external support. This caused the war in a number of ways:

☑ The USA intervened to support the South. President Truman sent warships to South Korea, and offered advisers a supplies. Without this, South Korea would not have been able to fight the war.

☑ Kim II-Sung (p.107) had asked for Stalin's support to invade the south in 1949, but he had refused. Kim II-Sung cou not launch an invasion without aid from the USSR or China. Even though Stalin gave permission in 1950, he made clear his troops would not fight in the conflict directly, and any reinforcements must come from China.

How did China cause the Korean War?

There were 3 main reasons China contributed to the outbreak of the Korean War (p.22).

☑ In 1949 the communists won the civil war in China, against Chiang Kai-shek's non-communist government. Chin became a communist country.

☑ Because of its policy of containment, the US had supported Chiang Kai-shek's efforts, trying to prevent China from turning Communist. This strategy failed when Chiang Kai-shek lost the civil war.

☑ When China became communist, America was scared communism would spread through Asia, as it believed in th domino theory (p.50). The USA was committed to ensuring communism did not take hold in South Korea.

DID YOU KNOW?

The Korean War was an 'all-terrain war'. This was because troops fought in mountains, swampland, open plains, and forests.

THE NORTH KOREAN INVASION OF SOUTH KOREA, 1950

'The people of the southern portion of Korea trust me and rely on our armed might. Partisans will not decide the question. The people of the south know that we have a good army. Lately I do not sleep at night, thinking about how to resolve the question of the unification of the whole country.'
Kim Il-Sung

What happened when North Korea invaded South Korea?

The Korean War *(p.22)* broke out when North Korea invaded South Korea and sent troops over the 38th parallel.

When did North Korea invade South Korea?

North Korea invaded South Korea on 25th June, 1950.

Why did North Korea invade South Korea?

North Korea invaded South Korea for 5 key reasons:

- ☑ North Korea invaded the south because Kim Il-Sung *(p.107)* wanted to unite Korea under communist rule. By June 1950, he was confident an invasion would be successful.
- ☑ Kim Il-Sung *(p.107)* had the support of communist leaders - Stalin in the USSR, and Mao Zedong in China.
- ☑ North Korea's armed forces were stronger than those of South Korea. The USSR had provided tanks, planes and heavy artillery.
- ☑ China became communist in 1949 and, after August that year, the USSR had the atom bomb. Kim Il-Sung *(p.107)* thought these factors would deter a US response.
- ☑ American politicians had made speeches suggesting Korea was not seen as a priority.

Why were North Korean troops able to invade South Korea so easily?

Very few American troops were available to help the South Koreans defend their territory, making it easier for the north to invade.

What was the significance of North Korea's invasion of South Korea?

North Korea's invasion of South Korea was significant because it triggered a large-scale conflict that would last for 3 years and become the first hotspot of the Cold War in Asia.

DID YOU KNOW?

Temperatures were so low in Korea that, in the winter of 1950, many soldiers in the UN force died from hypothermia and frostbite.

THE UNITED NATION'S RESPONSE TO THE INVASION

'If the UN cannot bring the crisis in Korea to an end then we might as well just wash up the United Nations and forget it.'
US Senator Tom Connally

What was the response of the United Nations to the invasion of South Korea by North Korea?

When North Korea invaded South Korea, the Security Council of the United Nations *(p.25)* met on the same day - 25th June, 1950.

What was the UN's decision about South Korea following the invasion?

In the days following the invasion of South Korea, the UN passed 3 resolutions on the matter:

- ☑ The first, on 25th June, called the invasion a 'breach of the peace' and called for North Korea to withdraw its troo
- ☑ The second, on 27th June, recommended that member nations of the UN should supply troops to stop the invasi
- ☑ The third, on 7th July, recommended the UN troops come under the command of the USA.

How did North Korea react to the United Nation's resolutions in response to the invasion of South Korea?

North Korea ignored the UN's first resolution, that ordered them to withdraw its troops.

Why did the UN support South Korea after they were invaded in 1950?

The UN was able to pass resolutions condemning North Korea because the USSR was not present. The Soviets were boycotting the UN because of the organisation's refusal to admit communist China as a member.

Which countries supplied troops for the UN in South Korea after the invasion?

Troops from the USA and 15 other countries, including Britain and France, were sent to assist South Korea. The USA supplied the majority of the support given.

DID YOU KNOW?

Korea was the first war in which the United Nations intervened.

THE USA'S RESPONSE TO THE INVASION

'If we let Korea down, the Soviets will keep right on going and swallow up one place after another.'
President Harry Truman, speaking after North Korea invaded South Korea, 25th June, 1950

What was America's response to the invasion of South Korea?

The USA put pressure on the United Nations *(p.25)* to condemn the North Korean invasion *(p.31)*. It took control of the subsequent UN invasion and supplied by far the largest number of troops.

Why did America defend South Korea during the invasion?

America had a number of reasons for wanting to defend South Korea, and for pressuring the UN to become involved

- ☑ It had been involved in establishing the Republic of Korea.
- ☑ It was determined, under its policy of containment, to prevent further communist expansion.
- ☑ It was concerned the invasion of South Korea might encourage a Chinese attack on Formosa (Taiwan) and lead to massive shift in world power from capitalism to communism.
- ☑ If the UN had failed to act, it is likely America would have taken action on its own to prevent this.
- ☑ Truman wanted to avoid the mistakes of the 1930s. There would be no appeasement and the USA would support t UN to ensure it did not fail as the League of Nations had.

How was the UN influenced by America in the invasion of South Korea?

The United Nations *(p.25)*' action in Korea was very much influenced by the USA.

Quizzes, amazing exam preparation tools and more at GCSEHistory.com

- ☑ The UN forces were commanded by General MacArthur, an American.
- ☑ Half the ground forces were American.
- ☑ America contributed more than 90% of the air forces.
- ☑ 85% of the naval forces were American.

Why did the USA's response to the invasion of South Korea lead to some people calling it 'America's war'?

Some people called the Korean War *(p.22)* 'America's war' for the following reasons:

- ☑ The amount of troops the USA sent to support UN forces - 302,483 soldiers in total. The UK sent the second highest number of troops, but that was only 14,198.
- ☑ An American, General MacArthur, led the UN army in Korea.
- ☑ It was widely known the forces took their orders from the USA rather than from the United Nations *(p.25)*.

DID YOU KNOW?

It was the USA that pushed the suggestion the UN should send an army to aid South Korea.

THE USSR'S RESPONSE TO THE INVASION

The United Nations was 'less concerned with peace than with supporting America in its open war against the Korean people.'
Andrei Gromyko, Soviet Foreign Minister.

What was the response of the USSR to UN intervention in the Korean War?

The USSR had given Kim Il-Sung *(p.107)* and North Korea permission to invade South Korea, whatever the UN's response.

What were the criticisms of the USSR about the UN intervention in the Korean War?

The USSR had several criticisms of the UN's intervention in the Korean War *(p.22)*:

- ☑ It argued the UN Charter did not permit the organisation to get involved in 'internal events'; the Soviets said the conflict between North and South Korea was such an event.
- ☑ It claimed to be committed to the UN's policy of non-intervention in other states' internal affairs, inferring the organisation's actions contravened its own charter.
- ☑ It said the aim of UN intervention was 'to deprive Korea of national independence and to transform the country into an American colony'.
- ☑ It stated that: 'Koreans have the same right to unify as was used by the northern American states in the American Civil War.'.

Why did the USSR have this response to the UN intervention in the Korean War?

The USSR felt the US had too much influence in the UN, and the USSR wanted to see a united Korea under communist rule.

THE UN CAMPAIGN IN SOUTH KOREA

'The issues are global and so interlocked that to consider the problems of one sector, oblivious to those of another, is to court disaster. While Asia is referred to as the Gateway to Europe, it is no less true that Europe is the Gateway to Asia, and the influence of the one cannot fail to have its impact upon the other.'
General MacArthur

What was the UN campaign in South Korea?

The UN's campaign in South Korea was to help the country's troops defend against the North Korean army, which had advanced quickly after its initial invasion on 25th June, 1950.

Who led the UN campaign in South Korea?

General Douglas MacArthur *(p.104)* was appointed chief of the UN forces in Korea and led the campaign.

Where was the UN campaign in South Korea?

The UN campaign began around the city of Pusan, which the North Koreans had reached. UN troops then launched a surprise attack from the sea, at the port of Inchon on South Korea's west coast. This was 160 kilometres below the 38th parallel, where Korea was divided, and 40 kilometres from Seoul, the South Korean capital.

Why was the UN campaign in South Korea important?

The UN campaign was important if the South Koreans were to have any chance of pushing back North Korean forces, which had advanced quickly. It aimed to stop the complete collapse of South Korea and was also the first test of the USA's policy of containment in Asia.

When was the UN campaign in South Korea?

The UN launched its campaign to push back the North Korean army in September 1950.

What were the key events in the UN campaign in South Korea?

There were 7 key events in the UN campaign in South Korea:

- ☑ On 14th September, Kim Il-Sung's *(p.107)* forces had pushed the South Korean army back to the area around Pusan.
- ☑ UN troops were sent in to defend Pusan.
- ☑ On 15th September, UN troops began a surprise attack from the sea at Inchon, a port on South Korea's west coast.
- ☑ Inchon was swiftly captured by the UN army, which then launched an offensive inland to retake Seoul.
- ☑ While some UN forces focused on the offensive towards Seoul, the remaining UN troops and the South Korean army began advancing north from Pusan.
- ☑ Both armies - the troops advancing towards Seoul and those going north - moved towards each other and were able to attack Kim Il-Sung's *(p.107)* army from both sides.
- ☑ By October, the North Korean troops had retreated back behind the 38th parallel.

What were the results of the UN campaign in South Korea.

The UN campaign, sometimes known as the 'Inchon landings', was very successful. Its forces managed to capture the port of Inchon quickly, and were also able to retake Seoul and advance north. Within a month, North Korean troops had been completely driven out of South Korea.

DID YOU KNOW?

Due to the significant involvement of American troops in the UN forces, many people refer to Korea as 'America's war'.

THE INCHON LANDING

An amphibious invasion that changed the fortunes of South Korea.

What was the Inchon Landing?

The Inchon Landing was a surprise attack by UN forces against the North Korean army.

When was the Inchon Landing?

The Inchon Landing started on 15th September and ended 4 days later, on 19th September, 1950.

Who was involved in the Inchon Landing?

The Inchon Landing involved 75,000 troops and 261 naval vessels. The operation was planned and led by General Douglas MacArthur *(p.104)*.

Where did the Inchon Landing happen?

The surprise amphibious invasion launched from the sea at the port of Inchon on South Korea's west coast, 40 kilometres from Seoul, the capital city.

What were the key events in the Inchon Landing?

There were 4 key events in the Inchon Landing:

- ☑ In September 1950, while the North Koreans believed the UN forces were fenced in, MacArthur started to withdraw troops from around the city of Pusan. He planned an amphibious attack on the port of Inchon.
- ☑ The UN forces took Wolmi, an island near Inchon, with few casualties.
- ☑ By nightfall on September 15, UN soldiers controlled Inchon. They then advanced on Seoul.
- ☑ By 27th September, UN troops that had been defending the area around Pusan joined with UN forces from the Inchon Landing. The North Korean army was devastated and, by 29th September, Syngman Rhee *(p.107)* was back in power in Seoul.

Why was the Inchon Landing carried out?

General MacArthur intended to use Inchon as a base to recapture Seoul, the South Korean capital, from North Korea.

What were the results of the Inchon Landing?

As a result of the Inchon Landing, UN forces managed to recapture Seoul and drove the North Korean troops back behind the 38th parallel.

What was the significance of the Inchon Landing?

The Inchon Landing was significant as it turned the fortunes of the Korean War *(p.22)* in the UN forces' favour. Its su
also turned MacArthur into a hero.

DID YOU KNOW?

The invasion was challenging and many advised against it. It was not timed
precisely, and as Inchon's tides fluctuate wildly, the area the soldiers planned to
cross by boat was a mudflat. Furthermore, MacArthur decided to invade in the
middle of typhoon season.

THE UN FORCES' ADVANCE INTO NORTH KOREA

'We hurled back the invader and decimated his forces. Our victory was complete and our objectives
within reach, when Red China intervened with numerically superior
ground forces.'
General MacArthur

What was the UN campaign in North Korea?

After pushing Kim Il-sung's *(p.107)* forces back into North Korea above the 38th parallel, the UN approved its own
soldiers to cross the border, driving the North Koreans further north.

Why did the UN continue their campaign in North Korea?

The United Nations *(p.25)* continued its campaign against Kim Il-Sung's *(p.107)* forces into North Korea for 2 key reaso

✅ It hoped to defeat Kim Il-Sung's *(p.107)* forces completely and achieve the reunification of South and North Korea
This had been the intention since the 2 nations were first divided.

✅ Although some people were worried about China entering the war, since it was a communist nation that bordere
North Korea, General MacArthur convinced US President Truman this would not happen.

What mistake did the UN make with the campaign in North Korea?

General MacArthur made the mistake of assuming China would not enter the war. When UN troops began pushing
North Korean forces towards the Yalu River on the Chinese border, 200,000 Chinese soldiers joined them to fight b

What were the results of the UN campaign in North Korea?

The UN had hoped to defeat the North Korean army and unite the two nations. However, when China entered the wa
the UN forces were pushed back into South Korea, and North Korea and China re-took Seoul.

DID YOU KNOW?

General MacArthur fought in the First World War and won 13 medals for his
bravery.

THE ENTRY OF CHINA TO THE KOREAN WAR

'War can only be abolished through war, and in order to get rid of the gun it is necessary to take up the gun.'
Mao Zedong

What happened when China intervened in the Korean War?

China entered the Korean War *(p.22)* after UN forces advanced north of the 38th parallel into North Korean territory.

When did China intervene in the Korean War?

In October 1950, approximately 200,000 well-equipped Chinese soldiers crossed the Yalu River into North Korea to help Kim Il-Sung's *(p.107)* troops.

Why did China intervene in the Korean War?

General MacArthur had wrongly predicted China would not get involved when UN forces advanced into North Korea. China got involved for 3 key reasons:

☑ China wanted to ensure North Korea remained communist and act as a buffer between Manchuria and US-backed South Korea.

☑ The USA had broken its promise not to cross the 38th parallel, so China was concerned the troops would continue advancing north and cross the Yalu river.

☑ When Stalin and President Mao of the People's Republic of China met in October 1950, Stalin encouraged Mao to act quickly to stop the UN forces' advance in North Korea.

What were the key events in China's intervention in the Korean War?

There were 5 key events in the Chinese intervention in the Korean War.

☑ As MacArthur led the UN troops further into North Korea and advanced towards the Yalu river, which ran across the Chinese border, President Mao warned China would join the war if they continued further.

☑ By the middle of October, MacArthur and the UN forces had almost destroyed the North Korean army and continued their advance north towards China's border. There is speculation MacArthur did this on purpose to provoke China.

☑ China launched a surprise attack on the UN soldiers; it had now officially entered the war.

☑ On 25th October, PRC forces attacked UN soldiers at Pukchin; on 1st November, they defeated UN troops at Unsan.

☑ The UN forces continued to face defeats into 1951, and by March they had been driven back below the 38th parallel into South Korea. Chinese and North Korean troops had re-captured Seoul.

What was the impact of China's intervention in the Korean War?

China's intervention had a negative impact on the UN's campaign in North Korea. The UN had successfully driven North Korean troops out of South Korea and almost destroyed Kim Il-Sung's *(p.107)* army. However, China's entry turned the tide of the war, and now the UN troops were on the retreat.

What was the response of the USA to China's intervention in the Korean War?

President Truman and General MacArthur responded very differently to China's intervention in the Korean War *(p.22)*.

☑ Truman was concerned about China's entry and felt 'containing' communism and successfully defending South Korea was a satisfactory outcome. There was no need to further antagonise China. He also believed a war with China would bring Stalin into the conflict, which could ultimately lead to the use of nuclear weapons.

☑ MacArthur was at odds with Truman's thinking. Even though Truman told him not to, he sent UN troops back into North Korea. He wanted a united Korea and wanted China to surrender. He believed the USA should use the nuclear bomb if it was necessary.

What were the results of China's intervention in the Korean War?

China's entry into the Korean War *(p.22)* had 3 key results:

☑ President Truman sacked General MacArthur.

☑ Truman had changed his strategy in Korea and wanted to limit the scale of the war.

☑ By March 1951 the Chinese advance had been halted, and UN forces recaptured Seoul. By the middle of 1951 there a stalemate; neither side could advance, and faced each other across the 38th parallel.

 What was the significance of China's intervention in the Korean War?

China's intervention in the Korean War *(p.22)* was significant as their actions drove back UN forces and led to a stalem Their entry also widened the scope of the Cold War in Asia, involving China in a more significant way.

DID YOU KNOW?

Manchuria, and especially Liaoning – the Chinese province north of the Yalu River – was China's most important industrial centre. As UN forces advanced closer to the border, China's entry to the war was therefore inevitable.

GENERAL DOUGLAS MACARTHUR AND THE KOREAN WAR

'I can almost hear the ticking of the second hand of destiny. We must act now or we will die.'
General MacArthur

 What did General Douglas MacArthur do in the Korean War?

At the age of 70, General Douglas MacArthur *(p.104)* was appointed chief of the UN task force sent to Korea in 1950. H played a significant role in the Korean War *(p.22)*.

 What were the key events General Douglas MacArthur was involved in during the Korean War?

The 8 key events of MacArthur's role in the Korean War *(p.22)* included:

☑ When MacArthur arrived in Korea, his first job was to stop the South Korean army being completely wiped out. H sent troops to defend the area around the city of Pusan.

☑ MacArthur then launched a surprise attack, called the Inchon Landings.

☑ Next, he led UN forces to recapture the city of Seoul, which had fallen to Kim Il-Sung's *(p.107)* North Korean army.

☑ By October 1950, MacArthur had successfully led the UN campaign to drive the North Korean army back to their homeland, behind the 38th parallel.

☑ MacArthur then launched an offensive into North Korea in the hope of reuniting Korea under capitalism. This we against recommendations not to do so, due to the concern China would join the war. However, MacArthur was confident Mao's troops would not attack.

☑ MacArthur's predictions were wrong, and he and his troops were pushed back into South Korea by the united forc of North Korean and Chinese soldiers.

☑ MacArthur was ordered by Truman not to go back into North Korea. He ignored this, saying he wanted to unite K and the USA should be prepared to engage in nuclear warfare if this is what it took.

☑ As a result of disregarding President Truman's orders, MacArthur was sacked in April 1951 and ordered to return the USA.

Why was General Douglas MacArthur sacked during the Korean War?

MacArthur was sacked because he disobeyed direct orders. There was real concern he might trigger a nuclear war. Some people felt he deliberately provoked China into entering the war by ignoring their warnings against advancing further north in Korea. He also repeatedly expressed a willingness to use nuclear weapons.

Who took over General Douglas MacArthur's role in the Korean War?

General MacArthur was replaced by Lieutenant General Matthew Ridgway.

What was the public reaction to General Douglas MacArthur being sacked during the Korean War?

MacArthur was a popular war hero in America and his sacking was condemned by the public. He received a hero's welcome on his return home.

What was the significance of General Douglas MacArthur's role during the Korean War?

MacArthur was a significant and controversial figure in the Korean War *(p.22)* for 5 main reasons:

- ☑ He was responsible for changing the tide of events, masterminding the Inchon Landing *(p.35)*, and was able to recapture South Korea at the start of the war.
- ☑ His actions led to China's involvement, which turned the tide again - but this time not in the UN's favour.
- ☑ He was sacked by President Truman for disregarding orders and was replaced by Lieutenant General Ridgeway.
- ☑ His attitude regarding nuclear warfare was heavily criticised. Some people felt there was a real danger of the conflict becoming a nuclear war and MacArthur was pushing towards this.
- ☑ He wrote a public letter criticising President Truman.

DID YOU KNOW?

There was a dispute between President Truman and General MacArthur during the Korean War. In a 1973 article in Time magazine, Truman was quoted as having said, off the record: 'I fired him because he wouldn't respect the authority of the president.'

THE MILITARY STALEMATE AROUND THE 38TH PARALLEL

'Over a period of three years or so, we killed off - what - twenty percent of the population of Korea as direct casualties of war, or from starvation and exposure.'
Curtis LeMay, general in US Air Force.

What was the stalemate in the Korean War?

By 1951, after many successes and failures on both sides, the Korean War *(p.22)* had reached a stalemate at the 38th parallel. Neither the UN forces, nor the Chinese and North Korean troops, could push the other back or gain a strategic advantage.

When did the stalemate in the Korean War happen?

The stalemate was reached in the middle of 1951, after the UN forces recaptured Seoul in March 1951.

Where did the stalemate happen in the Korean War?

The stalemate in the Korean War *(p.22)* took place along the 38th parallel. The UN forces were positioned in South Korea, and the Chinese and North Korean troops were positioned in North Korea.

How did UN forces try to break the stalemate in the Korean War?

In December 1951 the front line along the 38th parallel was holding steady, with both sides trying to break each oth[er's] heavily fortified positions. The USA took various actions in an attempt to end the stalemate and get North Korea to surrender.

- ☑ The USA decided to take advantage of its air power.
- ☑ They bombed North Korean villages, towns and cities, as well as transportation infrastructure, factories, and military assets.
- ☑ The USA used napalm in the bombings. Estimates suggest up to 1,000,000 people, including civilians, were kill[ed in] the campaign.

How did Chinese and North Korean forces try to break the stalemate in the Korean War?

Chinese and North Korean troops fought back in the air and battled with UN forces in the skies over Korea for almo[st 2] years.

How did the USSR get involved in the stalemate in the Korean War?

Stalin sent military equipment, ammunition, and Soviet fighter planes and pilots to support the Chinese and North Korean troops.

How did the USSR conceal its involvement in the stalemate in the Korean War?

Stalin only agreed to send aid to Chinese and North Korean troops as long as the USA would not find out. He was concerned about the possibility of direct confrontation between the USSR and America, and took steps to conceal h[is] nation's involvement.

- ☑ All Soviet planes were painted with Chinese or North Korean symbols.
- ☑ Stalin forbade Soviet pilots from speaking Russian on the radio.
- ☑ Soviet pilots wore Chinese uniforms.

What were the results of attempts to break the stalemate in the Korean War?

The battle in the air between both sides raged for almost 2 years. UN forces lost approximately 3,500 planes, while N[orth] Korea, China and the Soviets lost almost 3,000. However, neither managed to end the stalemate.

DID YOU KNOW?

Another famous military stalemate was along the Western Front during the First World War. It lasted 4 years.

THE PEACE TALKS AND THE GENEVA ACCORDS

The peace treaty that ended the Korean War put each side back exactly where it started at the beginning - either north or south of the 38th parallel.

What were the peace talks in the Korean War?

Neither side in the Korean War (p.22) could break the stalemate that occured along the 38th parallel. They therefore entered into peace talks to bring the conflict to an end.

Quizzes, amazing exam preparation tools and more at GCSEHistory.com

When did the peace talks happen in the Korean War?

Peace talks to end the conflict started in July 1951. However, due to problems with reaching an agreement, a peace treaty between the UN, China and North Korea was not signed until 27th July, 1953.

Why was there problems with the peace talks in the Korean War?

The peace talks faced a number of problems because the two sides disagreed on everything.

How did they come to an agreement during the peace talks in the Korean War?

Circumstances changed in both the USA and the USSR, which helped the two sides come to an agreement.

☑ Dwight D Eisenhower was elected President of the USA in 1952, replacing Truman. Eisenhower was keen to bring an end to the Korean War *(p.22)*.

☑ Joseph Stalin died in March 1953, and North Korea and China felt there would be limited support from a new Soviet leader. They had relied on the superior technology the Soviets had supplied for the war in the air.

What was agreed at the peace talks in the Korean War?

The peace talks reached some key conclusions.

☑ North Korea and South Korea would remain as independent nations.

☑ The border between the two countries would remain at the 38th parallel.

☑ A 3km-wide demilitarised zone was created between North and South Korea, to act as a barrier to prevent future conflict.

What was the result of the peace talks in the Korean War?

The peace talks led to the signing of an armistice. Although peace was not formally declared, the agreement did result in the end of fighting in Korea.

DID YOU KNOW?

Decades later, the truce remains all that technically prevents North Korea and the USA - along with South Korea - from resuming the war, as no peace treaty has ever been signed.

THE IMPACT OF THE KOREAN WAR

When thinking about the impact of war, the human cost is always the highest.

What was the impact of the Korean War?

The Korean War *(p.22)* lasted for just over 3 years. It resulted in a huge number of lives lost, and had a massive impact on US military spending, the United Nations *(p.25)*, and the Cold War *(p.16)*.

What was the impact of the Korean War on the USA's military spending?

The Korean War *(p.22)* led the USA to increase military spending. In 1953 it spent $30 billion, approximately 14 per cent of its gross domestic product (GDP).

What was the impact of the Korean War on the United Nations?

The Korean War *(p.22)* was the first time the UN played a role in conflict. Its quick action to defend a nation fighting a aggressor earned it great respect. Its position as a world-leading organisation was strengthened, helping it shake of poor reputation of its predecessor, the League of Nations.

What was the impact of the Korean War on the Cold War?

The Korean War *(p.22)* was the first conflict of the Cold War *(p.16)*, and as such affected it in a number of ways:

- ☑ With the Cold War *(p.16)* now spreading to Asia, the USA built alliances with countries around the region, includi the Philippines.
- ☑ The USA began to rebuild Japan, to prevent communism spreading there.
- ☑ The USA cut off relations with China, and threw its support behind the previous government that was now based Taiwan.
- ☑ The USA entered into an alliance with Australia and New Zealand, called the ANZUS pact, whereby all three nati promised mutual aid in the event of an invasion.
- ☑ The USA increased its commitment to fighting communism and increased support to other nations for this purp Between 1950 and 1954, America spent $3 billion helping France to keep control of Vietnam against communist rebels.
- ☑ In the context of the Cold War *(p.16)* it was a victory for the USA, as it had stopped the spread of communism. It w defeat for the USSR, who wanted the opposite.
- ☑ The war did not lead to the USA and the USSR resolving their differences; in fact, the opposite happened. The US, was more committed than ever to containing communism and both sides entered into an arms race, which inclu increasing their respective nuclear capabilities.

What was the impact of the Korean War with regard to lives lost?

The Korean War *(p.22)* was a bloody conflict. It is impossible to know exactly how many people died, but it is agreed t official human cost of the war was incredibly high for all nations involved:

- ☑ North Korea: 600,000 civilians killed or missing; 406,000 military personnel killed or missing; 1,500,000 milita personnel wounded.
- ☑ South Korea: 1,000,000 civilians killed or missing; 217,000 military personnel killed or missing; 430,000 militar personnel wounded.
- ☑ The USA: 36,600 military personnel killed or missing; 103,000 military personnel wounded.
- ☑ China: 600,000 military personnel killed or missing; 716,000 military personnel wounded.
- ☑ Other UN forces: 3,000 military personnel killed or missing; 12,000 military personnel wounded.

DID YOU KNOW?

The Korean War was the first war with battles between jet aircraft.

THE WEAPONS BUILD-UP

*By the 1950s, both the USA and the USSR had developed intercontinental ballistic missiles (ICBMs),
a terrifying new technology that allowed the long-range delivery and detonation of nuclear warheads.*

What was the weapons build-up during the Korean War?

The Korean War *(p.22)* had an impact on the military of both superpowers. Both the USA and the USSR began to spend increasing sums of money on military development, and on nuclear weapons in particular.

How much did the USA spend on the build up of their weapons during the Korean War?

The USA spent $48 billion in 1951, and $60 billion in 1952.

What did the USA military spend money on in the weapons build-up during the Korean War?

The USA military spent money on the following:

- ☑ 750 nuclear bombs, a vast increase on the 100 it had in 1948.
- ☑ Improving the technology of nuclear weapons.
- ☑ Increasing the US Army by 50 per cent, to 3.5 million troops.
- ☑ Increasing the number of military bases outside US territory in Europe, the Middle East and Asia.

What did the USSR military spend money on in the weapons build-up during the Korean War?

The USSR also increased its military spending. It improved its nuclear weapons with the introduction of intercontinental ballistic missiles (ICBMs). It also increased the size of its army, navy and air force.

DID YOU KNOW?

Neither the USA or the USSR had any idea about the other's nuclear arsenal. American politicians genuinely believed there was a 'missile gap' between them and the Soviets, and began stockpiling nuclear weapons.

THE VIETNAM WAR

The Vietnam War remains prominent in the minds and memories of the American people.

What was the Vietnam War?

The Vietnam War was a lengthy conflict which began in 1954, after Vietnam was divided into two. North Vietnam wanted to reunite the country under communism while South Vietnam, assisted by the USA, fought to keep this from happening.

When did the Vietnam War happen?

Officially the Vietnam War began in 1955 and ended in 1975. However, some events prior to 1955 are important in order to understand how the war developed.

What were the key phases in the Vietnam War?

There were 4 key phases to the Vietnam War, including:

- The 1st phase of the conflict was between 1945 and 1954. The Vietminh *(p.46)* fought to drive French imperial rule from Vietnam. This ended with the signing of the Geneva Accords and Vietnam being split into 2 countries. This period is called the First Indochina War *(p.47)*.

- The 2nd phase, between 1957 and 1963, saw the leader of South Vietnam, Ngo Dinh Diem *(p.100)*, fight a bitter civil war against the Vietcong *(p.58)* which was supported by Ho Chi Minh's *(p.105)* government in the north. This ended with Diem being assassinated just weeks before the American president, John F Kennedy, was assassinated in November 1963.

- The 3rd phase, from 1964 to 1968, saw a huge escalation in the conflict between America - which before 1964 had direct military presence in the region - and North Vietnam. America was fighting the Vietcong *(p.58)* directly in to stop a communist takeover in the south.

- The 4th phase of the conflict, between 1969 and 1973, was defined by America's desire to withdraw from Vietnam its actions to bring US troops home. The last military personnel were withdrawn from the region in 1973.

Who was involved in the Vietnam War?

There were a number of different parties and nations involved in the war including:

- France - the roots of the conflict begin with its attempts to maintain rule in Vietnam after the Second World War

- Ho Chi Minh's *(p.105)* Vietminh *(p.46)*, which fought to remove all foreign influences from Vietnam. After the divi of the country in 1954, under the Geneva Accords, Ho Chi Minh would become the leader of North Vietnam. Mu the war featured his battles with the Americans as he tried to take over South Vietnam and unite the two nation:

- The USA was involved in the conflict from July 1950, when it tried to assist the French against the Vietminh *(p.46*

- Both China and the USSR were involved, supporting Ho Chi Minh *(p.105)* from the start of conflict as he tried to out the French.

- South Vietnam was a new country created in 1954 under the Geneva Accords, and America's presence there was to stop a communist takeover.

- Cambodia and Laos were drawn into the conflict on occasions, due to shared borders with Vietnam.

What was the role of France in the Vietnam War?

From 1945, the French had fought to keep control of its colonies in Indochina. In Vietnam, over 50,000 French soldi had been killed as France fought against the Vietminh *(p.46)* for 8 years.

What was the background to the Vietnam War?

In 1954, a peace agreement was signed in Geneva between the French and the Vietnamese. Vietnam was divided into communist North Vietnam and US-backed South Vietnam. In 1960 a guerrilla organisation, the Vietcong *(p.58)*, was formed in the south. Its aim was to overthrow Diem *(p.61)*, the region's leader, and unite the whole of Vietnam under communist rule.

Why did the USA get involved in the Vietnam War?

The USA was concerned about the Domino Theory *(p.50)* and could not allow South Vietnam to become communist. became increasingly involved in supporting South Vietnam as part of its containment policy *(p.20)*.

How did the USA get involved in the Vietnam War?

There were 3 key stages to American involvement in the Vietnam War:

- From 1950, the USA gave $1.6 billion dollars in aid to South Vietnam, and sent political advisers.

- From 1960, it began to send military advisers to train the South Vietnamese Army.

- From 1965, it sent American combat troops to Vietnam and became fully involved in the war.

Which US presidents got involved in the Vietnam War?

The USA's involvement in Vietnam spanned 5 different presidents:

- President Truman, who started sending military aid to the French to fight the Vietminh *(p.46)*.

- ✅ President Eisenhower, who was the first to send military aid to the new South Vietnamese government in January 1955.
- ✅ President Kennedy *(p.103)*, who began increasing the number of US military advisors sent to Vietnam to train the ARVN - the South Vietnamese army.
- ✅ President Johnson *(p.102)*, who committed the first US boots on the ground to Vietnam in March 1965.
- ✅ President Nixon *(p.106)*, who led the withdrawal of all American troops from Vietnam.

Why did people protest against the Vietnam War?

One of the defining features of the Vietnam War was the anti-war movement that developed in the USA. Protesters objected to many aspects, including the cost, the rising number of deaths, atrocities committed by US soldiers, and the draft system *(p.72)*.

How did people protest against the Vietnam War?

Protests included mass rallies, sit-ins, and the burning of draft cards.

How did the Vietnam War affect the Cold War?

The Vietnam War had an impact on the Cold War *(p.16)* in 3 main ways:

- ✅ It was a humiliating defeat for the USA. The world's greatest superpower had been beaten by a small, under-equipped, yet committed guerrilla army. It influenced US involvement in future conflicts.
- ✅ It was a failure of the containment policy *(p.20)*, as Vietnam was now united under communist leadership. Laos and Cambodia followed suit in 1975.
- ✅ Ironically, it helped lead to greater cooperation between the superpowers, as the USA sought the Soviet Union's help in ending the war.

What was the cost of the Vietnam War?

The Vietnam War cost much more than anticipated - a total of $167 billion.

What were the reasons for the Vietnam War being unwinnable?

Many historians argue the Vietnam War was unwinnable for 9 key reasons:

- ✅ North Vietnam was determined to withstand the USA.
- ✅ The US military struggled to defeat the Vietcong's *(p.58)* guerrilla tactics.
- ✅ The war had to stay within limits if the USA was to avoid confrontation with China or the USSR.
- ✅ The Americans knew little about the country.
- ✅ Vietnamese peasants were alienated by American policy, and the tactics used by the US military.
- ✅ Vietnam had a history of opposing conquering countries, such as France and Japan.
- ✅ The USA was unable to close the Ho Chi Minh Trail *(p.59)*, which was used to supply the Vietcong *(p.58)*.
- ✅ American soldiers were unused to jungle warfare, while the Vietnamese were experts.
- ✅ The South Vietnamese government had been unstable ever since the death of Diem *(p.100)* in 1963.

DID YOU KNOW?

The war would eventually claim the lives of more than 58,000 Americans and some 3 million Vietnamese.

FRENCH RULE IN ASIA BEFORE THE SECOND WORLD WAR

'Your county belongs to the western seas, ours to the eastern. As the horse and buffalo defer, so do we – in language, literature, customs. If you persist in putting the torch to us, disorder will be long. But we shall act according to the laws of Heaven, and our cause will triumph in the end.'
Emperor Tu Duc to France's Admiral de Genouilly, 1857

What did France rule in Asia before the Second World War?

In the 1700s, during the age of empire building, France took control of significant parts of southeast Asia. This area known as French Indochina.

Where did France rule in Asia before the Second World War?

France ruled French Indochina, which included Cambodia, Laos and Vietnam.

Why did France extend its rule in Asia before the Second World War?

France built an empire in parts of southeast Asia for 3 main reasons:

- ☑ Much of the area, especially Vietnam, was rich in raw materials such as coal and zinc. France could sell these resources globally.
- ☑ Areas such as Vietnam had a large number of peasant farms France could use for agriculture.
- ☑ They could export goods made in France to sell to the colonies in southeast Asia.

What was the impact of the Second World War on France's rule in Asia?

The Second World War saw France occupied by the Nazis and impacted French Indochina in 3 key ways:

- ☑ Japan occupied French Indochina and took important raw materials from Vietnam, including spices, metals, coal rice. Japan plundered so much that 2,000,000 Vietnamese had died of starvation by 1945.
- ☑ The war led to the development of a strong resistance group called the Vietminh *(p.46)*, who wanted to remove all foreign rule from Vietnam.
- ☑ At the end of the Second World War the Vietminh *(p.46)* declared Vietnam's independence, and this led to bitter wa with France.

DID YOU KNOW?

The 5 colonial territories of French Indochina had become independent by 1954.

THE VIETMINH

'The Vietnamese people deeply love independence, freedom and peace. But in the face of United States aggression they have risen up, united as one man.'
Ho Chi Minh

What was the Vietminh?

The Vietminh was a Vietnamese resistance group. It was founded in 1941 during Japanese occupation in the Second World War.

Quizzes, amazing exam preparation tools and more at GCSEHistory.com

Who created the Vietminh?

The Vietminh was created and led by 2 communists, Ho Chi Minh *(p.105)* and Nguyen Vo Giap.

Why was the Vietminh created?

The Vietminh was created to drive all foreign rule out of Vietnam.

What actions did the Vietminh take when it was first created?

From the Second World War until 1954, the Vietminh took a number of key actions in an effort to drive foreign rule from Vietnam.

- ☑ It fought with Japan and, by 1945, had taken control of most of northern Vietnam.
- ☑ After being defeated, Japan left Indochina, including Vietnam.
- ☑ The Vietminh was keen to build on its success against Japan. In September 1945 they declared Vietnam an independent country, with Ho Chi Minh *(p.105)* as president. France was unhappy about this.
- ☑ France sent troops to fight the Vietminh, as it did not intend to allow Vietnam to be an independent country.
- ☑ The Vietminh fought against France until 1954.

DID YOU KNOW?

The two are sometimes confused and thought to be the same, but the Vietminh and Vietcong were two separate guerrilla organisations.

THE FIRST INDOCHINA WAR, 1946-1954

This was the Vietminh's attempt to drive French imperial rule out of Vietnam.

What was the First Indochina War?

When Ho Chi Minh *(p.105)* declared Vietnam was independent, naming it the Democratic Republic of Vietnam, fighting broke out between French troops and the Vietminh *(p.46)*. This part of the conflict is called the First Indochina War.

When did the First Indochina War happen?

The First Indochina War took place between 1946 and 1954.

Where did the First Indochina War happen?

The conflict was largely in the north of Vietnam, but on occasions the entire country was involved. It also spilled into other parts of French Indochina, including Laos and Cambodia, which bordered Vietnam.

What were the key events in the First Indochina War?

There were a number of key events in the First Indochina War.

- ☑ With the Vietminh *(p.46)* struggling against the better trained French soldiers, Ho Chi Minh *(p.105)* initially sought a peace deal. However, no agreement was reached.
- ☑ In November 1946, French troops took control of Hanoi in the north, forcing Ho Chi Minh *(p.105)* to retreat into the jungle.
- ☑ From 1950, China intervened in the war to help the Vietminh *(p.46)*.

- ☑ A turning point in the war came in 1954, with the Battle of Dien Bien Phu *(p.51)*.
- ☑ France was defeated at the Battle of Dien Bien Phu *(p.51)*, and the Geneva Agreement aimed to bring a peaceful resolution to the conflict.

What was China's involvement in the First Indochina War?

The communists won the civil war in China and took over in 1949. They wanted to help the communist Vietminh *(p.* and sent support in the form of training, and military supplies and equipment.

What was the USA's involvement in the First Indochina War?

The USA's involvement in the First Indochina war included:

- ☑ A commitment to support France in order to contain communism.
- ☑ $15 million in military aid, given by President Truman to France in 1950.
- ☑ US planes, tanks and other military supplies sent to support the French.
- ☑ A total of $3 billion spent to support French efforts to keep control in Vietnam.

Why did the USA get involved in the First Indochina war?

American foreign policy was dictated by ideas such as the policy of containment and the Domino Theory *(p.50)*. The wanted to stop the Vietminh *(p.46)*, which they saw as China's 'puppet', and to stop communism spreading in southe Asia.

What tactics did the Vietminh use in the First Indochina War?

The Vietminh *(p.46)* used guerrilla tactics in the war. An example is what was known as 'hit-and-run'. The Vietminh soldiers launched offensives from their hideouts in the dense jungle where the French could not find them, attackir quickly and then returning to their positions. This tactic killed over 80,000 French troops.

What problems did the French face in the First Indochina war?

The French found it challenging to fight against the Vietminh's *(p.46)* guerrilla warfare, and often they made the situ worse by attacking peasant villages. This led to a rise in support for their enemy, Ho Chi Minh *(p.105)*.

DID YOU KNOW?

The war is also known as the Anti-French Resistance War.

TRUMAN'S WAR

President Truman's actions marked the beginning of America's involvement in Vietnam.

What was Truman's involvement in Vietnam?

America's extensive involvement in Vietnam begun under the presidency of Harry Truman *(p.108)*, who provided Fra with support to maintain rule in the region.

When did President Truman get involved in Vietnam?

President Truman first became involved in Vietnam in July 1950, when he sent France $15 million in military aid to them fight against the Vietminh *(p.46)*.

Why did President Truman get involved in Vietnam?

Under the Truman Doctrine *(p.19)*, President Truman committed to assist any country under threat of a communist takeover. At the time the USA was fighting a war in Korea through the proxy of a UN task force. Truman became concerned the French would be defeated by the communist Vietminh *(p.46)* and communism would then spread throughout Asia.

What was the significance of President Truman's involvement in Vietnam?

President Truman's role in Vietnam was significant due to the obligation it created to the region. Once he committed support to Vietnam this continued under each consecutive president. While each had doubts about further committing the USA, neither did they want to be the president who lost Vietnam to communism.

DID YOU KNOW?

Officials in Asia warned Harry Truman that French rule of Vietnam would lead to 'bloodshed and unrest'.

EISENHOWER'S WAR

'The purpose of this offer is to assist the government of Vietnam in developing and maintaining a strong country, capable of resisting attempted aggression through military means.'
President Dwight Eisenhower

What was President Dwight Eisenhower's involvement in Vietnam?

Eisenhower was one of 5 US Presidents to get involved in Vietnam. While he did not want to commit actual US boots on the ground, ie soldiers, he wanted to support the ARVN and contain communism in Vietnam.

When was Eisenhower involved in Vietnam?

Eisenhower was involved in Vietnam throughout much of his presidency. In July 1953 he took steps to end the fighting in Korea, but in January 1955 he sent the first shipment of military support to Saigon, the capital of South Vietnam.

Why did Eisenhower get involved in Vietnam?

There were 4 main reasons Eisenhower increased financial and military support and sent military advisers to South Vietnam:

- ☑ It was Eisenhower who first coined the term 'Domino Theory *(p.50)*'. He was incredibly concerned about the spread of communism in Asia.
- ☑ He was further convinced of the need for greater involvement when China and the USSR backed Ho Chi Minh's *(p.105)* communist North Vietnam.
- ☑ He saw Vietnam as an escalation of the Cold War *(p.16)*.
- ☑ There was growing support from the American public for increasing involvement in Vietnam due to the Red Scare, or fear of communism.

What influenced Eisenhower's policy in Vietnam?

Whilst Eisenhower wanted to prevent the spread of communism in Asia, equally he did not want to spend too much money on military overseas rather than investing in domestic policies at home.

What were the key events in Eisenhower's involvement in Vietnam?

EIsenhower's involvement in Vietnam involved political, military and financial measures. There were 9 key events between 1953 - 1961:

- ☑ Eisenhower refused to aid the French at the Battle of Dien Bien Phu *(p.51)*, which resulted in France's defeat by the Vietminh *(p.46)* and surrender in the war.
- ☑ He played a role in negotiating the Geneva Accords in 1954.
- ☑ In January 1955 he sent the first shipment of aid to the newly created South Vietnam.
- ☑ He allowed South Vietnam to join SEATO (Southeast Asia Treaty Organisation). The organisation's purpose was t co-ordinate efforts to stop the spread of communism in Southeast Asia. It was created in September 1954 and oth members included Britain, France, Australia, New Zealand and Pakistan.
- ☑ He began sending military advisors to train the ARVN in 1954.
- ☑ In 1954 he sent CIA spies to Saigon, in South Vietnam, to gather intelligence.
- ☑ He did not follow the agreements made at the Geneva conference by allowing Diem *(p.100)* to hold elections in Sou Vietnam in 1956.
- ☑ He gave Diem's *(p.100)* regime money, supplies and military equipment to fight the National Liberation Front in th civil war.
- ☑ He tried to encourage Diem *(p.100)* to carry out land reform in South Vietnam in an effort to boost his popularity amongst the South Vietnamese people.

What was the significance of Eisenhower's involvement in Vietnam?

Eisenhower's involvement in Vietnam was significant because it marked a turning point in US policy. While he did n commit troops to fighting in Vietnam, he did become more involved - making it difficult to pull back.

DID YOU KNOW?

Eisenhower didn't think it wise to spend money on fighting international conflicts at the expense of domestic reforms at home. But, like his successors, he became sucked into the affairs of Vietnam.

THE DOMINO THEORY

'You have a row of dominoes set up, you knock over the first one, and what will happen to the last one is the certainty that it will go over very quickly. So you could have a beginning of a disintegration that would have the most profound influences.'
President Dwight Eisenhower

What was the Domino Theory?

The Domino Theory said that if one country fell under communist influence, the surrounding nations in that region would also fall - like a line of dominos.

When was the Domino Theory created?

The phrase 'Domino Theory' was first used in 1954.

Who came up with the Domino Theory?

The phrase was first used by US President Eisenhower when he suggested the fall of French Indochina to communism could result in a domino effect in south east Asia.

Quizzes, amazing exam preparation tools and more at GCSEHistory.com

What started the idea of the Domino Theory?

The idea of the 'Domino Theory' was a consequence of the Cold War *(p.16)*. The 3 main causes were:

- ✅ The US government had committed to limiting the spread of communism in Europe through the Marshall Plan. The idea was that communism would take root in poorer countries, so supporting those nations' economies would stop the spread.
- ✅ The USA witnessed communist takeovers in some Asian countries including China, North Korea, and North Vietnam.
- ✅ Eisenhower believed Ho Chi Minh *(p.105)* wanted all of Vietnam to become communist, and that if this happened communism would spread to Laos, Cambodia, Thailand, Burma, Malaysia, Indonesia and India. Vietnam was the first 'domino'.

What was the impact of the Domino Theory on the USA?

The fear triggered by the Domino Theory impacted the USA in 5 key ways:

- ✅ People began to believe there were Soviet spies living among American people and plotting to overthrow the government.
- ✅ The House Un-American Activities Committee (HUAC) was established to investigate suspected communist spies.
- ✅ Some filmmakers were accused of spreading communist propaganda.
- ✅ The McCarran Act was passed. This legislation restricted employment for communists and stipulated that all communist organisations had to be registered and investigated.
- ✅ It led to something called the Red Scare, a paranoia about communism, which facilitated McCarthyism. This in turn led to an increase of public support for greater involvement in Vietnam.

DID YOU KNOW?

While Truman recognised the danger of a ripple effect of communist takeovers in Asia, it was Eisenhower who articulated the idea of countries in Asia falling like dominos.

DIEN BIEN PHU AND ITS CONSEQUENCES

This major turning point saw the Vietminh successfully drive French imperial rule out of Vietnam.

What was Dien Bien Phu?

Dien Bien Phu was a decisive battle between French and North Vietnamese troops in 1954.

When did Dien Bien Phu take place?

The Battle of Dien Bien Phu was fought for 57 days between 13th March and 7th May, 1954.

Who was involved at Dien Bien Phu?

France fought the Battle of Dien Bien Phu against North Vietnam and the Vietminh *(p.46)*.

What was the result of Dien Bien Phu?

There were 5 significant results of Dien Bien Phu.

- ✅ France lost the battle.

- [x] Over 3,000 French soldiers were killed and 8,000 were wounded.
- [x] The Vietminh *(p.46)* lost 8,000 troops and a further 12,000 were wounded.
- [x] It was a massive humiliation for the French.
- [x] The remaining French soldiers were made to march to prisons located far away, with many dying during the jou...

Why did Dien Bien Phu happen?

The French felt one last large battle would defeat the communists.

How were the French defeated at Dien Bien Phu?

The French were defeated for 6 main reasons:

- [x] The 10,000 French soldiers defended an airfield known as Dien Bien Phu, which was in a valley.
- [x] The French were surrounded and had their supplies cut off by 50,000 Vietminh *(p.46)* soldiers.
- [x] The Vietnamese were willing to use suicide bombers.
- [x] The Vietnamese managed to get artillery to the top of the surrounding hills and bombarded Dien Bien Phu.
- [x] They launched attacks with vast numbers of men and were willing to take heavy casualties.
- [x] The French ran out of essential supplies like water and medicines. Although they asked for help, neither the USA Britain would come to their aid. The French surrendered on 7th May, 1954.

Why did the French surrender at Dien Bien Phu?

The French surrendered at Dien Bien Phu for 3 key reasons:

- [x] They had been defeated in the battle.
- [x] They could not secure support from outside parties such as Britain and the USA.
- [x] The French parliament voted 471 to 14 in support of ending the war and withdrawing from French Indochina.

What were the consequences of Dien Bien Phu?

The defeat at Dien Bien Phu had 2 important consequences.

- [x] It ended France's 8-year war with the Vietminh *(p.46)*.
- [x] Over 400,000 soldiers and civilians lost their lives in the First Indochina War *(p.47)*.

DID YOU KNOW?

By 1954, the USA was supplying 80% of the equipment being used by the French. However, when supplies ran out at Dien Bien Phu, the Americans refused to help.

THE GENEVA ACCORDS, 1954

The Geneva Accords divided Vietnam along the 17th parallel.

What were the Geneva Accords?

The Geneva Conference was a meeting between 9 countries which focused on resolving the war between France and Democratic Republic of Vietnam. The agreements that were reached became known as the Geneva Accords.

When was the Geneva Conference?

The Geneva Conference took place from 26th April to 21st July, 1954.

Who attended the Geneva Conference?

Representatives of 9 countries attended the Geneva Conference:

- ☑ Cambodia.
- ☑ Laos.
- ☑ China.
- ☑ France.
- ☑ Britain.
- ☑ USSR.
- ☑ USA.
- ☑ Vietminh *(p.46)* (North Vietnam).
- ☑ The State of Vietnam (South Vietnam).

Where was the Geneva Conference held?

The conference was held in Geneva, Switzerland.

Why was the Geneva Conference held?

The Geneva Conference was held to bring a peaceful end to the conflict in Indochina.

What was agreed by the Geneva Accords?

The Geneva Accords resulted in numerous important agreements regarding Vietnam:

- ☑ Vietnam was split into two on a temporary basis, with a demilitarised zone in the middle. The country was divided at the 17th parallel, which was approximately halfway down.
- ☑ The south would be run by Emperor Bao Dai, who had spent a lot of time in the USA and strongly opposed communism.
- ☑ The north would be controlled by Ho Chi Minh *(p.105)*, a communist.
- ☑ France had to withdraw from Vietnam.
- ☑ The Vietminh *(p.46)* had to withdraw from the south.
- ☑ The Vietnamese could choose if they wanted to live in the north or the south.
- ☑ Elections were to be held in 1956 to decide who ruled the whole of Vietnam. However, no clear electoral system was agreed.
- ☑ No foreign forces would be allowed to set up military bases in Vietnam.
- ☑ There were 300 days of free movement. One million people moved south; 130,000 moved north; and 5,000 to 10,000 supporters of North Vietnam stayed in the south.
- ☑ Laos and Cambodia were created.

What was the USA's response to the Geneva Accords?

President Eisenhower was worried about the spread of communism in the region and was committed to containing it. The USA refused to sign the accords, but became more involved in the future of Vietnam. In January 1955, America sent a shipment of military aid to Saigon, the capital of South Vietnam, and offered to train the new army.

What was the response of South Vietnam to the Geneva Accords?

South Vietnam refused to sign the accords. Diem *(p.100)*, the prime minister, did not want to accept the division of the country as he wanted a united Vietnam.

What was the response of North Vietnam to the Geneva Accords?

China forced North Vietnam to agree to the demands, even though it would have a smaller area of control than in 19 Ho Chi Minh *(p.105)* wanted a united country, but he believed the division would only be temporary as the people of Vietnam would vote for a communist government in the elections that were due to be held before July 1956.

DID YOU KNOW?

The Geneva conference also discussed two other Cold War hotspots - Berlin and Korea.

NGO DINH DIEM'S GOVERNMENT IN SOUTH VIETNAM

'Oh, he's a great anti-communist - it's just that he finds the Buddhists are easier to get at.'
Caption from a cartoon by American Herbert Lawrence Block, an open critic of the Diem regime

What was Diem's government?

In 1954 Ngo Dinh Diem *(p.100)* became Prime Minister of a US-backed government in the Republic of Vietnam, or Sou Vietnam. Many reports show Diem's government used violence and nepotism to rule the country.

Why was Diem's government chosen by the USA to govern South Vietnam?

Diem *(p.100)* was chosen by the USA because he was anti-communist. He had studied in America and the US authoriti thought they could control him. America believed he was the best chance of containing communism in North Vietna and stopping its spread throughout south east Asia.

What problems were there with Diem's government?

There were 4 key problems with Diem's *(p.100)* government that led to significant opposition:

- ☑ Diem *(p.100)* did not follow the advice given by America, and many of his decisions upset the USA.
- ☑ He gave peasants' land to powerful families and important jobs to his friends and family.
- ☑ He implemented unfair taxes.
- ☑ Those who opposed Diem's *(p.100)* government were imprisoned and some were even murdered.

What did Diem's government do to break the Geneva agreement?

A key agreement at Geneva was the holding of an election for the whole of Vietnam by July 1956. However, Diem *(p.10* held his own election in South Vietnam in October 1955. Anyone who disagreed with it was arrested.

What did Diem's government do in the elections?

There were 2 candidates in the elections: Diem *(p.100)*, and Bo Dai, the former emperor of Vietnam. With America's he Diem used 3 main tactics to secure victory:

- ☑ Dai's name was printed on a green background on the ballot paper, while Diem's *(p.100)* name had a red backgroun The colour red is associated with good luck in Vietnam.

☑ People who looked as if they would vote for Dai were intimidated.

☑ Diem *(p.100)* inflated the percentage of those who had voted for him to 98 per cent.

Who opposed Diem's government in South Vietnam?

There were two main groups of opposition to Diem's *(p.100)* rule in South Vietnam:

☑ The National Liberation Front, a political movement comprising different groups brought together by Ho Chi Minh *(p.105)*.

☑ Members of the Buddhist religion.

Why did the National Liberation Front oppose Diem's government?

The National Liberation Front wanted to unite North and South Vietnam, and replace Diem's *(p.100)* government with one that was representative of all groups in South Vietnam, not just the Catholics favoured by Diem.

How did the National Liberation Front oppose Diem's government?

The National Liberation Front used violence. It targeted members of the government and hundreds of people were murdered. Ho Chi Minh *(p.105)* told the NLF to target the Army of the Republic of Vietnam (ARVN).

Why did Buddhists oppose Diem's government?

Buddhists opposed Diem's *(p.100)* government for 4 main reasons:

☑ Diem *(p.100)* was a Catholic and favoured Catholics in society. He often gave them important positions in government.

☑ The majority of Vietnamese people were Buddhists, but Diem *(p.100)* adopted anti-Buddhist policies.

☑ Buddhists had to have permission from the government to worship.

☑ 9 Buddhists, 8 of whom were children, were killed when troops shot them for flying the official Buddhist flag during a celebration.

How did Buddhists oppose Diem's government?

Buddhists opposed Diem's *(p.100)* government using methods such as hunger strikes, mass rallies, and gaining support from the foreign press. In one protest a monk called Thich Quang Duc burned himself alive, while monks and nuns handed out flyers that urged Diem's regime to show kindness to other religious groups.

What were the consequences of opposition to Diem's government?

Diem's *(p.100)* corrupt and brutal regime led many of his opponents to believe a revolution was the only way to change things, and civil war broke out in South Vietnam in 1957.

DID YOU KNOW?

Diem's ancestors were among the first Vietnamese who converted to Roman Catholicism.

THE CIVIL WAR IN SOUTH VIETNAM

The opposition against Diem's regime reached tipping point and resulted in a civil war.

What was the civil war in South Vietnam?

In 1957, after growing opposition to Diem's *(p.100)* government in South Vietnam, people left their homes and move the jungle to form armed resistance groups.

When did the civil war in South Vietnam happen?

The civil war in South Vietnam broke out in 1957, and ended with the murder of Diem *(p.100)* in November 1963.

Where did the civil war in South Vietnam happen?

The civil war was fought across South Vietnam, with much of the fighting taking place in the jungle. Supply lines fc NFL ran along the borders of Vietnam, Laos and Cambodia. This became known as the Ho Chi Minh Trail *(p.59)*, and was an important part of the war.

Who was involved in the civil war in South Vietnam?

The civil war in South Vietnam was fought between Diem *(p.100)* and the ARVN (South Vietnamese Army), supporte the USA, against the National Liberation Front, which was funded by Ho Chi Minh *(p.105)* in North Vietnam.

Why was there a civil war in South Vietnam?

The civil war broke out as an attempt to overthrow Diem's *(p.61)* regime, due to its brutality and corruption. Many Sc Vietnamese people saw the government as cruel; Madame Nhu, the First Lady of South Vietnam, celebrated when t Buddhist Quang Duc set himself on fire and called it a 'barbecue'.

What role did the USA play in the civil war in South Vietnam?

The USA was desperate to keep Diem *(p.100)* in power in order to stop the spread of communism. America supported Diem during the civil war.

- ✅ The USA gave the ARNV weapons, fighter jets, and helicopters.
- ✅ It gave $1.6 billion of financial aid to South Vietnam in the 1950s.
- ✅ It sent advisers to train ARVN soldiers on how to fight the NLF.
- ✅ It used propaganda to try and turn people against communism. It said the Vietminh *(p.46)* and the Chinese were killing civilians in South Vietnam, including those who opposed communism in the north.

How did the civil war in South Vietnam end?

By 1961 the USA realised how unpopular Diem *(p.100)* was, and withdrew its support. With no protection, Diem fell victim to a coup. He was captured by ARVN generals on 1st November, 1963, and shot the next day.

DID YOU KNOW?

Every election held during Diem's rule was corrupt. In the October 1954 referendum, where people were asked to vote on a republican political system, Diem recorded more than 600,000 votes in Saigon; the electoral roll had only 450,000 people.

Quizzes, amazing exam preparation tools and more at GCSEHistory.com

KENNEDY'S WAR

'No greater task faces this country or this administration. No other challenge is more deserving of our every effort and energy. Too long we have fixed our eyes on traditional military needs, on armies prepared to cross borders, on missiles poised for flight. Now it should be clear that this is no longer enough - that our security may be lost piece by piece, country by country.'
President John F Kennedy

What was President Kennedy's involvement in Vietnam?

John F Kennedy *(p.103)* was reluctant to commit US troops to Vietnam, and instead wanted to send military advisors and financial aid to support the ARVN in its fight against communism.

When was Kennedy involved in Vietnam?

Kennedy *(p.103)* inherited Eisenhower's legacy in Vietnam, so was involved from the start of his presidency in 1961 until his assassination in 1963.

Why did Kennedy get involved in Vietnam?

Kennedy *(p.103)* got involved in Vietnam for 3 key reasons:

- ✅ He was very interested in foreign policy.
- ✅ Kennedy *(p.103)* was committed to Eisenhower's 'Domino Theory *(p.50)*' and the policy of containment. In 1947 he had voted in favour of the Truman Doctrine *(p.19)*.
- ✅ When Kennedy *(p.103)* took office in 1961 the Cold War *(p.16)* was accelerating, with tensions rising between the USA and the USSR.

What influenced Kennedy's involvement in Vietnam?

Kennedy *(p.103)* had an extensive domestic programme to deal with at home, and wanted to avoid the financial burden of large-scale military support in Vietnam.

What were the key events in Kennedy's involvement in Vietnam?

There were 6 key events in Kennedy's *(p.103)* involvement in Vietnam:

- ✅ He sent approximately 16,000 military experts to train the ARVN. This was more than Eisenhower committed during his presidency.
- ✅ Kennedy *(p.103)* was conscious of public opinion and kept the increased US presence in Vietnam a secret.
- ✅ By the end of 1961 the ARVN had increased from 150,000 to 170,000 troops, as a result of funding from Kennedy *(p.103)*.
- ✅ He sanctioned the coup by the ARVN to remove Diem *(p.100)* from power. Diem was murdered on 1st November, 1963, just weeks before Kennedy *(p.103)* was assassinated.
- ✅ He sent 300 US helicopter pilots to South Vietnam, under orders not to engage with the enemy. However, it became increasingly difficult not to as the Vietcong *(p.58)* shot at them.
- ✅ He endorsed the Strategic Hamlet programme *(p.60)* in Vietnam.

What was the significance of Kennedy's involvement in Vietnam?

Kennedy's *(p.103)* involvement in Vietnam was significant as he increased the USA's commitment to the region. Building on Eisenhower's interventions, it would make it very difficult for the next president to scale back.

DID YOU KNOW?

President Kennedy was assassinated just weeks after Diem was killed in South Vietnam.

THE VIETCONG

'You will kill ten of us, we will kill one of you, but in the end you will tire of it first.'
Ho Chi Minh

What was the Vietcong?

The Vietcong (VC) was made up of over a dozen different political and religious groups based in South Vietnam. The
opposed the South Vietnamese government, both politically and militarily.

When was the Vietcong established?

The Vietcong was established on 20th December, 1960.

Who was the leader of the Vietcong?

The leader of the Vietcong was Hua Tho. Although he was non-communist, so were many members of the organisati

Why was the Vietcong established?

The Vietcong was formed for three main reasons:

☑ There was much anger and frustration at Diem's *(p.100)* failure to hold the elections agreed at the Geneva Confere
which would have meant a united Vietnam.

☑ Frustration pushed some people to violence, and groups of South Vietnamese people intended to use terror tactic
force elections or overthrow Diem's *(p.61)* regime.

☑ The violence resulted in many members of Diem's *(p.100)* government being murdered. He hit back by sending the
ARVN into the jungle to hunt down rebel forces. A report produced by Ho Chi Minh's *(p.105)* advisor, Le Duan,
commented that Diem's policy was proving successful, and therefore the rebel forces in South Vietnam had to
become more organised.

What was Ho Chi Minh's involvement with the Vietcong?

Le Duan's report convinced Ho Chi Minh *(p.105)* that he needed to help the resistance fighters in the south if they wer
be successful. He persuaded different armed groups who opposed Diem *(p.100)* to come together in one organisation –
National Liberation Front, or the Vietcong, as it was called by the ARVN and US advisers.

What were the aims of the Vietcong?

The Vietcong had 3 key aims.

☑ It wanted to overthrow Diem *(p.61)* and establish a new government that represented all groups in South Vietnam
society.

☑ It was committed to the reunification of Vietnam, independent of all foreign influence.

☑ It was committed to the redistribution of wealth and restoration of peasants' rights.

Who supported the Vietcong?

The Vietcong had both domestic and international support.

☑ Domestic support for the Vietcong was vast. As well as communists, and nationalists who wanted reunification, i
appealed to the middle classes, teachers, doctors, and also peasants and workers.

☑ Internationally, the Vietcong was supported by North Vietnam, China and the USSR.

How was the Vietcong supported by the North?

The North developed various supply routes to help the Vietcong, including the Ho Chi Minh Trail.

How did the Vietcong fight?

The Vietcong used 4 guerrilla tactics against Diem's *(p.100)* ARVN forces.

☑ Their aim was not to destroy, but to wear down.

☑ They fought in cells of 8-10 soldiers.

☑ They blended into the population, making it difficult for Diem's *(p.100)* forces to find them.

☑ They picked their battles, attacking at night and only fighting if they outnumbered enemy soldiers.

What was the difference between the Vietcong and the Vietminh?

The Vietminh *(p.46)* was the anti-Japanese and anti-French force created in the 1940s to drive out foreign colonialists. After the division of Vietnam, its members resided in the north. The Vietcong was created in the 1950s to fight Diem's *(p.100)* regime in the south, and was used as North Vietnam's vehicle for creating chaos across the south.

What was the Ho Chi Minh Trail which was used by the Vietcong?

There are 4 important details to note about the Ho Chi Minh Trail:

☑ It was a supply route from North to South Vietnam.

☑ It was a series of parallel roads that ran along the Vietnamese border, often through thick jungle.

☑ The route went from North Vietnam, through Laos and Cambodia, to South Vietnam.

☑ It was used to send supplies, troops and weapons to the Vietcong.

What did the Vietcong do to gain help and support?

The Vietcong used both positive and oppressive methods to control the Vietnamese.

☑ They used violence and intimidation to control villages.

☑ They created a political group called the National Liberation Front (NLF). It spread communist ideas among the villages, and encouraged people to help the Vietcong.

How did President Kennedy try to defeat the Vietcong?

President Kennedy *(p.103)* sent an extra 16,000 advisers to South Vietnam, to train the Army of the Republic of Vietnam (ARVN) to fight the Vietcong. They were called 'advisers' rather than troops, because he wanted to avoid full-scale war.

What were President Kennedy's motives towards the Vietcong?

President Kennedy *(p.103)* wanted to stop communism and destroy the Vietcong.

Why did President Kennedy fail to defeat the Vietcong?

President Kennedy's *(p.103)* attempt to defeat the Vietcong failed for 3 main reasons:

☑ Efforts by US troops to train villagers to fight the Vietcong were unsuccessful because the Americans could not speak Vietnamese.

☑ The US troops were unable to stop the Vietcong visiting the villages at night, once they had left.

☑ The USA supported the ARVN, which was regarded as part of Diem's *(p.100)* corrupt government.

Why did the USA see the Vietcong as a threat?

The Vietcong was seen as a threat by the USA for 5 significant reasons:

☑ Although the ARVN had five times as many troops, it was too concerned over who should lead rather than pulling together to defeat the Vietcong.

☑ China supported the Vietcong by using the Ho Chi Minh Trail to send $100 million in aid to South Vietnam.

☑ The South Vietnamese government was seen as the USA's puppet and remained unpopular.

- ☑ The introduction of reforms, and the use of propaganda, meant the Vietcong gained local support.
- ☑ The number of attacks by the Vietcong increased and were focused on US military targets.

What was President Johnson's response to the Vietcong threat?

After President Kennedy *(p.103)* was assassinated, President Johnson *(p.102)* increased the number of US advisers in Vietnam to 20,000. He wanted to avoid US involvement in an escalating war by ensuring the establishment of a democratic and popular government that would oppose communism.

What was another name for the Vietcong?

US personnel referred to the Vietcong as 'Charlie'. This was because it was known as 'VC', which in the phonetic alp. is 'Victor Charlie'.

How did the Vietcong react to US intervention?

In the early 1960s, the Vietcong began 2 main projects to counter increasing US intervention:

- ☑ The amount of supplies brought along the Ho Chi Minh Trail was increased.
- ☑ It increased the number of guerrilla attacks, from 50 in September, 1961, to 150 in October.

Why did the Vietcong become more dangerous to the USA?

There were 3 main reasons why the Vietcong threat increased:

- ☑ Increasing tensions with the Americans had pushed the Vietcong to use more violent methods.
- ☑ America was increasing supplies, troops and operations in South Vietnam.
- ☑ However, the South Vietnamese were still unable to hold elections.

DID YOU KNOW?

The Vietcong was made up of people from both North and South Vietnam.

THE STRATEGIC HAMLET PROGRAMME

'The Strategic Hamlet Program failed because of over-expansion and the establishment of hamlets in basically insecure areas.'
From the Pentagon Papers

What was the Strategic Hamlet programme?

The Strategic Hamlet programme was an initiative introduced by Diem *(p.100)*, supported by President Kennedy *(p.10* and the US government that saw around 5,000 new villages built in South Vietnam.

When was the Strategic Hamlet programme introduced?

The Strategic Hamlet programme began in March 1962.

Why was the Strategic Hamlet programme introduced?

There were 3 key reasons the programme was introduced.

- ☑ Diem *(p.100)* was a very unpopular leader and it was an attempt to 'win the hearts and minds' of the South Vietna population.

Quizzes, amazing exam preparation tools and more at GCSEHistory.com

☑ Diem *(p.100)* portrayed it as a policy that helped the South Vietnamese people defend themselves against the Vietcong *(p.58)*.

☑ The hidden reason for the programme was to stop the Vietcong *(p.58)* using peasant villages for food and shelter. They also wanted to stop the Vietcong from gathering intelligence about the ARVN from the peasants.

How did the Strategic Hamlet programme work?

The programme worked by moving peasants away from their homes to new villages known as 'strategic hamlets'. These were surrounded by ditches and barbed wire. In just one year, between 1962 and 1963, two thirds of South Vietnamese people were forced to live in strategic hamlets.

How did the USA hope to gain support with the Strategic Hamlet programme?

It was hoped measures such as building new schools and hospitals, as part of the Strategic Hamlet programme, would build strong support for Diem *(p.100)*.

Why did the Strategic Hamlet programme fail?

The Strategic Hamlet programme failed for 4 key reasons:

☑ The new villages needed inhabitants, so people were forced to move into them even if they didn't want to.

☑ Many villagers believed they should live where their ancestors were buried, so the move upset them for religious reasons.

☑ Other peasants did not want to have to travel further to reach their rice fields.

☑ Not enough food was provided by the government, which meant some of those in the new hamlets faced starvation.

What were the consequences of the Strategic Hamlet programme?

The Strategic Hamlet programme had two key consequences:

☑ The programme made people less likely to support Diem *(p.100)*, not more. Membership of the National Liberation Front and the Vietcong *(p.58)* increased by 300% in two years.

☑ Its failure led Kennedy *(p.103)* to increase the USA's involvement in Vietnam, and he sent more military advisors to support Diem *(p.100)* and the ARVN.

What was the role of the Strategic Hamlet programme in the Hearts and Minds initiative?

'Hearts and Minds' was an American pacification programme, designed to persuade the South Vietnamese to reject communism. The Strategic Hamlets Programme was one aspect of it.

DID YOU KNOW?

The programme was hugely corrupt. Promised compensation for resettled peasants often found its way to the pockets of South Vietnamese government officials.

THE END OF DIEM'S GOVERNMENT
The end of Diem's rule in South Vietnam

What led to the overthrow of the Diem government?

Diem's *(p.100)* government became increasingly unpopular.

What were the events that led to the overthrow of the Diem government?

The overthrow of the Diem government *(p.54)* was the result of 4 key events:

- ✅ The loss of the Battle of Ap Bac, despite enormous support from the US military.
- ✅ In May 1963, Diem's *(p.100)* troops opened fire on a Buddhist procession and killed nine people.
- ✅ In June 1963, a Buddhist monk named Thich Quang Duc burned himself to death in Saigon as a protest against Di *(p.100)* treatment of Buddhists. Diem responded by ordering Buddhist temples to be raided and closed.
- ✅ America announced publicly it would no longer support Diem *(p.100)* and his government.

What was the result of the overthrow of the Diem government?

Diem *(p.100)* was removed from power by ARVN generals and later assassinated.

How was the USA involved in the overthrow of the Diem government?

While the USA was not directly involved with Diem's *(p.100)* assassination, there was evidence it was aware of the plc and made no move to prevent it due to Diem's unpopularity and instability.

Who took over after Diem was overthrown?

After Diem *(p.100)* was removed from power, South Vietnam was ruled by a series of military leaders until Nguyen Va Thieu became president in 1967.

DID YOU KNOW?

Kennedy sanctioned the coup against Diem as he recognised continuing to support him would not ultimately bring a satisfactory outcome.

JOHNSON'S WAR

President Lyndon B Johnson was the president who sent ground troops into Vietnam. He said, famously: 'I am not going to lose Vietnam. I am not going to be the president who saw Southeast Asia go the way China went.'

What was President Johnson's involvement in Vietnam?

Johnson's *(p.102)* intentions for Vietnam mirrored that of his predecessors, Eisenhower and Kennedy *(p.103)*. He did no want to commit combat troops. However, under Johnson's leadership, the USA's involvement greatly increased and i often for his role in Vietnam that Johnson is best remembered.

Why did President Johnson get involved in Vietnam?

There were 4 main reasons why Lyndon B Johnson *(p.102)* got involved in Vietnam:

- ✅ Like many American presidents of the Cold War *(p.16)* era, he firmly believed in Eisenhower's Domino Theory *(p.5* and was anxious about the spread of communism in Asia.
- ✅ Johnson *(p.102)* began his time in office following in Kennedy's *(p.103)* footsteps, and was only willing to commit military advisers to South Vietnam. However, his advisers wanted him to become more involved.
- ✅ Historian Arthur Schlesinger argued that Johnson *(p.102)* (as well as Kennedy *(p.103)*) escalated involvement becaus what he called the 'quagmire theory'. A quagmire is a soft boggy area of land that gives way underfoot; Schlesinge argued this was how Johnson's actions in Vietnam could be viewed.

☑ Other historians have argued that Johnson *(p.102)* did not want to be seen as the president that 'lost' Vietnam to communists, as Truman had 'lost' China. Johnson did not want the Democrats to be seen as 'soft on communism'.

What influenced Johnson's involvement in Vietnam?

Two key factors influenced Johnson's *(p.102)* involvement in Vietnam in the early years of his presidency:

☑ Johnson *(p.102)* had to win an election in 1964. He did not want to alienate the electorate, and believed a more peaceful appoach to the situation in Vietnam would win him public support.

☑ Many presidents of the Cold War *(p.16)* era had to balance the economic costs of domestic and foreign policy. Johnson *(p.102)* wanted to create a 'Great Society' that was fair to everyone in America, and such an ambitious domestic programme would require extensive funding. He was worried about the cost of further involvement in Vietnam.

Why did Johnson's advisers want him to get more involved in Vietnam?

His advisers, including US Secretary of Defence Robert McNamara, did not think the ARVN could defeat the Vietcong *(p.58)*. However, he believed if North Vietnam was attacked, Ho Chi Minh *(p.105)* would stop helping the organisation.

What were the key events in Johnson's involvement in Vietnam?

There were a number of key events in Johnson's *(p.102)* involvement in Vietnam:

☑ He approved Operation Plan 34A in August 1964.

☑ On 3rd August, 1964, North Vietnam attacked the USS Maddox which was stationed in the Gulf of Tonkin *(p.64)*.

☑ On 4th August, 1964, Johnson *(p.102)* launched a retaliatory act on North Vietnam. This became known as the Gulf of Tonkin *(p.64)* Incident.

☑ On 7th August, 1964, the Gulf of Tonkin Resolution *(p.64)* was passed.

☑ In February 1965 the Vietcong *(p.58)* attacked Camp Holloway, a US helicopter base in South Vietnam.

☑ On 13th February, 1965, the USA launched Operation Rolling Thunder *(p.65)*.

☑ By the end of 1965 there were 200,000 US combat troops in Vietnam, increased from 3,500 at the beginning of the year. Many see this as the start of the conflict.

☑ By 1967, Johnson's *(p.102)* administration was spending $30 billion a year on the war in Vietnam.

☑ In October 1967, over 100,000 people protested at the Lincoln Memorial in Washington against America's involvement in Vietnam.

☑ On 30th January, 1968, the North Vietnamese army and the Vietcong *(p.58)* launched a series of attacks. This became known as the Tet Offensive *(p.74)* - a significant turning point in the war.

☑ On Saturday, 16th March, 1968, 80 soldiers from the US military's 'Charlie Company' massacred over 300 innocent civilians in the village of My Lai in South Vietnam.

What was the significance of Operation Plan 34A in Johnson's involvement in Vietnam?

Operation Plan 34A involved sending South Vietnamese mercenaries into North Vietnam, and US naval ships into North Vietnamese waters in the Gulf of Tonkin *(p.64)*. This marked a key turning point, as it was a huge increase in the USA's involvement in the region, and it led to the Gulf of Tonkin incident.

What was the significance of Johnson's involvement in Vietnam?

Johnson's *(p.102)* involvement in Vietnam was significant for 3 key reasons:

☑ At first Johnson *(p.102)* followed the pattern of presidents before him. He increased US presence in Vietnam, with military advisors and support for the ARVN. However, his role was significant because his policies sent US troops to the region.

☑ US Secretary of Defence Robert McNamara stated that, in 1963, the military did not anticipate being in Vietnam for long and expected the withdrawal of 16,000 military advisers by the end of 1965. However, by the end of that year, Johnson *(p.102)* had committed 200,000 combat troops to the region.

☑ Johnson's *(p.102)* administration, and the president personally, faced mounting criticism from the American public about US involvement in Vietnam. The peace movement grew rapidly.

THE GULF OF TONKIN

'For all I know, our navy was shooting at whales.'
President Lyndon B Johnson

What was the Gulf of Tonkin Incident?

The Gulf of Tonkin incident occurred when three North Vietnamese torpedo boats fired on the USS Maddox, an American warship.

When was the Gulf of Tonkin Incident?

The Gulf of Tonkin incident happened on 2nd August, 1964.

Where did the Gulf of Tonkin Incident happen?

It happened in the Gulf of Tonkin, off the east coast of North Vietnam.

Why did the Gulf of Tonkin Incident happen?

Under Operation Plan 34A, South Vietnamese mercenaries were sent into the north. They were supported by US destroyer naval ships positioned in the Gulf of Tonkin, which were North Vietnamese waters. Ho Chi Minh *(p. 105)* w unhappy about this and launched the attack.

What were the key events in the Gulf of Tonkin Incident?

There were a number of key events in the Gulf of Tonkin Incident:

- ☑ The USS Maddox was sent to support the South Vietnamese mercenaries.
- ☑ On 3rd August, 1964, three North Vietnamese torpedo boats travelled towards the Maddox.
- ☑ The Maddox fired at the torpedo boats, which fired back. One torpedo hit but didn't explode.
- ☑ The US jets sank one torpedo ship and damaged the other two.
- ☑ On 4th August there was confusion over further attacks from North Vietnam. However, it was a false alarm; non had taken place.
- ☑ Despite the false alarm, Johnson *(p. 102)* sanctioned an attack on North Vietnam.

What were the consequences of the Gulf of Tonkin incident?

As a result of the incident, Johnson *(p. 102)* looked to scale up the USA's involvement in Vietnam. However, he first ne powers to do so, so he asked the US government to pass legislation called the Gulf of Tonkin Resolution.

What was the Gulf of Tonkin Resolution?

On 7th August, 1964, the US Congress passed the Gulf of Tonkin Resolution. This gave President Johnson *(p. 102)* permission to send troops to Vietnam and initiate further attacks on North Vietnam, without gaining permission fr Congress or formally declaring war.

What was the significance of the Gulf of Tonkin incident?

The Gulf of Tonkin incident was significant because it provided the opportunity for the USA to escalate its response in Vietnam. Some historians believe it was just an excuse, and the attacks never happened.

DID YOU KNOW?

When Congress passed the Gulf of Tonkin Resolution, there were only two dissenting votes. It was passed by the House of Representative 414-0, and got through the Senate by 88-2.

OPERATION ROLLING THUNDER

The USA's first major bombing campaign against North Vietnam.

What was Operation Rolling Thunder?

Operation Rolling Thunder was a mass bombing campaign on North Vietnam by the USA.

When did Operation Rolling Thunder happen?

Operation Rolling Thunder began in February 1965. Although it was only supposed to go on for eight weeks, it lasted three years.

Why did Operation Rolling Thunder happen?

Operation Rolling Thunder happened for 3 main reasons:

- ✅ US bases in South Vietnam had suffered a number of attacks from the Vietcong *(p.58)*, who were growing stronger thanks to supplies and support from North Vietnam.
- ✅ The trigger for the operation was the Vietcong *(p.58)* attack on the US base, Camp Holloway, which killed 8 American soldiers and injured hundreds more.
- ✅ A bombing campaign was chosen because the US thought it would cost fewer lives than ground warfare.

What was the aim of Operation Rolling Thunder?

The bombing campaign targeted government buildings, with the objective of breaking the North Vietnamese government's morale and prompting an end to its support for the Vietcong *(p.58)*.

How did Operation Rolling Thunder change over time?

To begin with, cities such as Hanoi and Haiphong were not attacked as Johnson *(p.102)* did not want to provoke the USSR and China by bombing civilians. However, this policy changed and the Americans switched to saturation, or carpet, bombing.

How did the USSR respond to Operation Rolling Thunder?

Operation Rolling Thunder led to a change of Soviet policy over Vietnam. After witnessing the damage caused by US bombs, it started to supply North Vietnam with anti-aircraft missiles with which it could fight back.

What was the significance of Operation Rolling Thunder?

Operation Rolling Thunder was significant as it was a huge escalation of US involvement in Vietnam.

THE TACTICS OF THE VIETCONG

The Vietcong's tactics were extremely important in fighting the superior technology of the US Army.

What tactics did the Vietcong use?

The US army was one of the largest, strongest, most advanced, and well-equipped armies in the world. In order to be it, and the ARVN, the Vietcong *(p.58)* had to use local jungle knowledge and guerrilla warfare to overcome their enem technology and defeat them.

What guerrilla warfare tactics were used by the Vietcong?

The Vietcong *(p.58)* used 6 main guerrilla warfare tactics to fight the US army and the ARVN:

☑ Soldiers did not wear uniforms, so its members could hide in plain sight among peasants. It was very hard to tell them apart from ordinary civilians.

☑ It had no headquarters and operated in small, well-armed groups, making it difficult to find them.

☑ It repurposed US mines by digging them up and creating booby traps, adding bamboo spikes and crossbows.

☑ It followed the rule of retreating when the enemy attacked, and attacking when the enemy retreated.

☑ It never attacked directly, instead picking off the enemy in ones and twos. Vietcong *(p.58)* members were famous fo disappearing quickly into tunnels before the enemy had a chance to react.

☑ It constantly attacked enemy camps.

What was the aim of the Vietcong tactics of guerrilla warfare?

The aim of guerrilla warfare was to create fear and break down the morale of the US forces.

What did Ho Chi Minh say about the Vietcong tactics of guerrilla warfare?

Ho Chi Minh *(p.105)* said the following:

☑ 'We must not go in for large-scale battles and big victories, unless we are certain of success.'.

☑ 'The aim of guerrilla warfare is to nibble at the enemy, harass him in such a way that he can neither eat nor sleep i peace, to allow him no rest, to wear him out physically and mentally.'.

☑ 'Wherever the enemy goes, he should be attacked by our guerrillas, stumble on land mines, or be greeted by snipe fire.'.

What were the typical features of a guerrilla fighter that used Vietcong tactics?

Vietcong *(p.58)* fighters shared a number of typical features and attributes:

☑ They had extensive knowledge of the local jungle which helped them ambush the enemy.

☑ They wore everyday civilian clothes so US forces could not identify them.

☑ They usually carried Soviet AK-47 assault rifles. This was a simple weapon to use but very accurate, and it could weather the watery terrain of the jungle.

☑ They travelled light with small rations of rice, enabling them to move quickly through the jungle.

☑ They would have tools to make 'punji sticks', which they used to make booby traps.

What was the Ho Chi Minh Trail that the Vietcong used in its tactics?

The Ho Chi Minh Trail *(p.59)* was a 600-mile route of many roads running through the thick jungle of Laos and Cambodia, parallel to the length of Vietnam. Supplies were sent along it from North Vietnam and China to South Vietnam. At the height of the war, 60 tons of equipment a day and 20,000 soldiers a month were transported.

What was important about the Ho Chi Minh Trail to Vietcong tactics?

The Ho Chi Minh trail *(p.59)* was incredibly important. It meant North Vietnam could ensure fighters in the south received regular supplies of weapons, food, and soldiers.

Why did the Vietcong tactic of using the Ho Chi Minh trail make it difficult for the enemy?

The US forces and the ARVN found the Ho Chi Minh *(p.105)* trails difficult for 2 main reasons:

☑ The trail was well organised. By the end of the war, you could travel the route from North Vietnam to Saigon in six weeks. The trail was 15,000 km long, and both US forces and the ARVN found it hard to overcome the challenges it posed.

☑ The US tried bombing the trail. However, when one section was bombed, the Vietcong *(p.58)* simply used a different section.

What was the idea of 'hanging on the belts' of Americans as a tactic of the Vietcong?

The idea was that the Vietcong *(p.58)* remained close to the enemy and engaged in close-quarter fighting. This helped them carry out surprise attacks and ambushes. As the Vietcong stayed so close it made bombing campaigns more difficult, as the Americans did not want to kill their own soldiers.

How were the tunnels used as a tactic by the Vietcong?

The tunnel system allowed the Vietcong *(p.58)* to move across South Vietnam without being seen, rather than risking being a target from the air. The tunnels were widely used as bases, ambush spots, and hospitals and also helped with the 'hanging on the belts of Americans' tactic.

What were the key features of the tunnels the Vietcong used as a tactic?

There were 3 key features of the tunnel systems:

☑ They were complicated systems that ran for over 300km beneath the Vietnamese jungle.

☑ They included kitchens, hospitals, sleeping quarters and meeting rooms, as well as storerooms for food, weapons, and explosives.

☑ They had various defence measures including hand-detonated mines at the surface, trap doors, air-raid shelters, booby traps, blast walls, false tunnels with booby traps, punji traps, tripwires, and remote smoke outlets.

What was the tactic of booby traps used by the Vietcong?

The Vietcong *(p.58)* used 6 main types of booby traps:

☑ Punji sticks.

☑ Snake pits.

☑ Grenade-in-a-can bombs.

☑ Flag bombs.

☑ Cartridge traps.

☑ 'Bouncing Betty' bombs.

How did the Vietcong use the booby trap punji sticks as a tactic?

The Vietcong *(p.58)* sharpened bamboo stakes, hiding them in shallow pits and covering them with leaves. The stake would pierce the enemy's boots and sever limbs. Sometimes they smeared the spikes with human excrement to infe the casualty's wounds.

How did the Vietcong use the booby trap snake pits as a tactic?

The Vietcong *(p.58)* guerrillas often carried bamboo pit vipers in their packs, to kill any enemy who searched them. T also tied snakes to bamboo sticks and placed them in their tunnel systems. When the bamboo was released, the sna was freed and would attack the enemy.

How did the Vietcong use the booby trap grenade-in-a-can bombs as a tactic?

Two cans were placed on trees, opposite each other. After removing the safety pins, grenades were placed in the can tripwire was then attached to each grenade. When the wire was tripped by the enemy, the grenades would be pulled of the cans and explode immediately.

How did the Vietcong use the booby trap flag bombs as a tactic?

US troops often captured enemy flags, so, when the Vietcong *(p.58)* left a base or location it would rig its flags with explosives.

How did the Vietcong use the booby trap cartridge traps as a tactic?

It was hard to detect cartridge traps, which made them terrifying. A cartridge - a round of ammunition - was placed inside bamboo and then put in a shallow hole in the ground. At the bottom of the bamboo was a board and a nail. Th weight of the enemy on the cartridge caused the nail to act as a firing pin, shooting the bullet upward into the victim foot.

How did the Vietcong use the booby trap 'Bouncing Betty' bombs as a tactic?

These traps would launch into the air when triggered and explode approximately 1m above the ground - at the heigh the stomach or genitals.

How many casualties were caused by the Vietcong's booby trap tactics?

The Vietcong's *(p.58)* traps caused around 19% of US casualties.

How was the organisation of the Vietcong part of its tactics?

The Vietcong *(p.58)* was organised in small groups called cells. Fighters rarely saw anyone outside their cell, so they couldn't betray the wider group if they were captured.

How did the Vietcong use disguise as part of its tactics?

Vietcong *(p.58)* fighters dressed as normal villagers, so US soldiers couldn't tell them apart from civilians. This led to of ordinary people losing their lives.

What were the Vietcong's tactics regarding the peasants?

The Vietcong *(p.58)* worked to get the support of the peasants in 4 key ways:

- ✅ They rarely attacked peasants or their property.
- ✅ They seized land from the wealthy and redistributed it among the poor, providing food and supplies.
- ✅ However, they were known to kill those who refused to support them. Between 1966 and 1971, 27,000 civilians we killed by the Vietcong *(p.58)*.

✅ They used propaganda to convince people they were beating the US Army. This included images of women and children, to show that everyone was helping to rid Vietnam of the Americans.

What were the successes of the Vietcong's tactics?

The Vietcong's *(p.58)* tactics were successful in 2 main ways:

✅ The aim of the tactics was to 'get inside the heads' of American soldiers and scare them, which they did.

✅ As a result of their tactics, the Vietcong *(p.58)* was able to use American weapons against them. In 1964, a report stated that 90 per cent of Vietcong weapons were US weapons that had been captured in ambushes.

What were the failures of the Vietcong's tactics?

The Vietcong's *(p.58)* tactics failed for 3 main reasons:

✅ Many civilians were mistaken as Vietcong *(p.58)* troops and killed.

✅ Not all Vietnamese people supported the actions of the Vietcong *(p.58)*, as terror and intimidation was sometimes used to gain local support.

✅ The guerrilla attacks alone were not enough to get rid of the Americans from Vietnam.

DID YOU KNOW?

Vietcong tactics were so successful they killed over 900 US soldiers on the first day of their duty in Vietnam, and around 1,400 troops on the day they were due to leave.

THE USA'S TACTICS AGAINST THE VIETCONG IN VIETNAM

'One does not use napalm on villages and hamlets sheltering civilians if one is attempting to persuade these people of the rightness of one's cause.'
An American's comment on US policy in Vietnam

What tactics did the USA use in the Vietnam War to fight against the Vietcong?

The USA had one of the most feared armies in the world as it was well trained and well equipped. But the USA's military resources were no match for the Vietcong's *(p.58)* guerrilla warfare. The US had to alter its tactics against the Vietcong as the war progressed.

What kind of soldiers did the USA send to combat the Vietcong's tactics in Vietnam?

When the war started the USA sent experienced GIs, or general infantryman, to fight against the Vietcong *(p.58)*. However, as fatalities and casualties piled up they increasingly sent younger, less experienced troops.

What was a GI, sent by the USA to combat Vietcong tactics in Vietnam?

American soldiers in the Second World War started calling themselves GIs, which stood for 'general infantryman'. The nickname became popular during the conflict in Vietnam. GIs faced many challenges there, which hampered America's ability to defeat the Vietcong *(p.58)* and win the war.

What were the typical features of a US soldier fighting against Vietcong tactics in Vietnam?

American GIs had 10 typical features or attributes:

✅ By the end of the war, the average age of a GI was 19.

- ☑ Many of the soldiers were forced to fight in Vietnam as part of military conscription, known as the draft. Soldier had to serve for a one-year period known as a 'tour of duty'.
- ☑ Unlike the Vietcong *(p.58)*, American GIs didn't travel light. They carried ration packs, ammunition, spare uniforr and as much water as they could. No matter how much water they carried, it was never enough to quench the thi caused by the climate of the Vietnamese jungle.
- ☑ The GIs' uniforms often rotted in Vietnam's hot, damp climate.
- ☑ GIs were often overzealous and made careless mistakes when out on patrol. They were often killed by the Vietcor *(p.58)* booby traps.
- ☑ Many GIs came from urban cities in the USA. Many had never travelled before and were ill-prepared for the environment and culture of Vietnam.
- ☑ They carried smoke grenades, to let US helicopters know when and where to extract them from the jungle.
- ☑ They carried fragmentation, or frag, grenades. When they exploded these sprayed red-hot fragments. However, many GIs were themselves accidentally killed by them, as the grenades often got caught on jungle plants.
- ☑ Unlike the Soviet AK-47 rifles used by the Vietcong *(p.58)*, the MI6 rifles carried by American GIs often jammed n water and mud, which was not ideal in Vietnamese jungle terrain.
- ☑ GIs wore boots with drainage holes to let the water out, and reinforced soles to combat the punji traps.

What methods did the USA use to combat Vietcong tactics in Vietnam?

The USA employed a number of tactics to fight against the Vietcong *(p.58)* guerrillas:

- ☑ 'Search and destroy', in which the US troops would enter Vietcong *(p.58)* territory, search out the enemy, and destr them.
- ☑ Bombing campaigns, such as Operation Rolling Thunder *(p.65)*.
- ☑ The use of explosive technology, such as pineapple bombs.
- ☑ The use of chemical warfare, including napalm and Agent Orange.
- ☑ The USA fought a war of attrition.
- ☑ The use of helicopters.

What was the 'search and destroy' tactic used by the USA to fight against the Vietcong in Vietnam?

Search and destroy was a US military tactic that worked in the following ways:

- ☑ Bases were built that stretched all along the South Vietnamese coast and border, to launch 'search and destroy' missions into the jungle.
- ☑ American forces searched villages for the Vietcong *(p.58)*. When they found the enemy they burned down the enti village, which destroyed the Vietcong base and served as a warning to other villages not to harbour the guerrillas
- ☑ This tactic soon earned the name 'zippo raids', as Zippo cigarette lighters were used to set fire to the thatched roo village houses.

What was Operation Cedar Falls in the USA's fight against Vietcong tactics in Vietnam?

Operation Cedar Falls was an example of 'search and destroy'. In 1967, 750 Vietcong *(p.58)* were killed. Despite early successes, the guerrillas soon returned. The level of violence created 4 million refugees, which increased the unpopularity of the South Vietnamese and USA.

Why was the USA's tactic of 'search and destroy' a failure fighting against Vietcong tactics in Vietnam?

The USA's tactic of 'search and destroy' failed for a number of reasons:

- ☑ US soldiers were simply not cut out to cope with the Vietcong's *(p.58)* guerrilla tactics.
- ☑ America's superior technology of heavy weapons and aircraft were better suited to open combat, but the Vietcong *(p.58)* did not engage with that method of fighting.
- ☑ As US troops searched for the enemy they were taken by surprise and attacked. The Vietcong *(p.58)* fighters would disappear back into the jungle before the Americans could respond.

- ☑ Young and inexperienced GIs could not tell the difference between Vietcong (p.58) soldiers and innocent villagers, and killed many ordinary civilians.

How did the USA use Operation Rolling Thunder to fight against Vietcong tactics in Vietnam?

Operation Rolling Thunder (p.65) was a major bombing campaign that lasted 3 years. It was an important US tactic.

- ☑ B-52 bombers dropped millions of tonnes of explosives.
- ☑ It targeted the Ho Chi Minh Trail (p.59) and industrial targets but not Hanoi, the capital of North Vietnam. As the campaign progressed, targets also included towns and cities in South Vietnam, and Vietcong (p.58) bases in Laos and Cambodia.
- ☑ It cost the USA $4 billion, and killed 90,000 people.
- ☑ President Johnson (p.102) wanted to bomb the Vietcong (p.58) into submission.

Why did the tactics used by the USA in Operation Rolling Thunder fail against the Vietcong in Vietnam?

There were 2 main reasons the bombing tactics of Operation Rolling Thunder (p.65) failed:

- ☑ Supplies continued to get through to the Vietcong (p.58) via the extensive tunnel system and the Ho Chi Minh Trail (p.59).
- ☑ Destroying industry didn't have an effect, as China and the USSR were sending military supplies to North Vietnam.

How did the USA use 'pineapple bombs' to fight against Vietcong tactics in Vietnam?

The USA developed a new weapon called the 'pineapple bomb', which exploded in the air and released 500 smaller bombs that caused huge damage. It was developed to maim rather than kill, so when someone was wounded, others would help - taking their attention away from the battle.

How did the USA use chemical weapons to fight against Vietcong tactics in Vietnam?

When the bombing campaigns failed to defeat the Vietcong (p.58), the Americans started to use chemical weapons. The 3 most widely used were:

- ☑ Agent Orange, a toxic weed killer used to destroy the jungle so the Ho Chi Minh trail (p.59) could be seen from the air.
- ☑ Agent Blue, a weed killer used to destroy crops so the Vietcong (p.58) would have no food.
- ☑ Napalm, a combustible chemical used to destroy the jungle.

What tactics were used by the USA in Operation Ranch Hand to fight against the Vietcong in Vietnam?

Operation Ranch Hand saw 3,000 villages sprayed with chemicals across 24% of South Vietnam. Water supplies were poisoned. There were some fatalities and many ongoing health problems.

What were the problems with the USA's use of chemical weapons to fight against Vietcong tactics in Vietnam?

The use of chemical weapons was inhumane. Agent Orange and Agent Blue led to people developing cancer and caused birth defects in newborns. Napalm burned through victims' skin, muscle and bone.

How did the USA use attrition warfare against the Vietcong tactics in Vietnam?

The US tactic of attrition meant focusing on killing as many Vietnamese soldiers as possible. It is estimated that around 1 million North Vietnamese and Vietcong (p.58) soldiers died, compared to 55,000 Americans. However, this tactic did not bring success for the US.

How did the USA use helicopters to fight against the Vietcong tactics in Vietnam?

Helicopters were used in 3 key ways.

- ☑ They were used to bring troops to a battle zone quickly, over difficult terrain.
- ☑ They supported ground troops during 'search and destroy' missions.
- ☑ They were used to evacuate wounded soldiers.

What were the successes of the USA's tactics used to fight against the Vietcong in Vietnam?

Overall, the US Army had little success. They did damage some of the supply lines along the Ho Chi Minh trail (p.59). However, the trail was so extensive it made little difference, making it impossible for the US to gain a strategic advantage in the war.

What were the failures of the USA's tactics to fight against the Vietcong in Vietnam?

Not only did US tactics result in the capture of very few Vietcong (p.58), their tactics alienated ordinary people. Man innocent people were killed, and the local people turned to the Vietcong due to the tactics employed by the US force Their use of chemical warfare was also condemned around the world for its abuse of human rights.

DID YOU KNOW?

The USA dropped more bombs on Vietnam than it had dropped in the whole of human history previously.

THE DRAFT SYSTEM

'Hell no, we won't go!'
A popular slogan opposing the draft system

What was the draft system for the Vietnam War?

Any man aged over 18 could be drafted into compulsory military service. Most were under 26, and the average was x years of age.

What training did people who were drafted into the Vietnam War receive?

Draftees received only basic training before being sent to fight in Vietnam.

What was the response to the draft system in the Vietnam War?

Many people felt the draft was unfair, that the draftees were too young, and that a lack of proper training increased chances of them dying.

What was the lottery system of the draft in the Vietnam War?

In 1969, to try and make the system fairer, the government turned the draft into a random lottery system. Men aged from 25 to 31 were included, adding a further 26 million potential soldiers. Out of 2.6 million men who fought in Vietnam, 650,000 were draftees.

Was anyone exempt from the draft in the Vietnam War?

4 main groups were exempt from the draft:

- ☑ The physically and mentally unfit.
- ☑ University students.
- ☑ Some government and industrial workers.

✅ Only sons, or those who could prove being drafted would create hardship for their families.

How many men were made exempt from the draft in the Vietnam War?

In total, 15 million men were made exempt from the draft.

What were the views of conscientious objectors on the draft for the Vietnam War?

Men could become conscientious objectors (COs) and refuse military service on the grounds of their religious or moral beliefs.

What work did conscientious objectors do as part of the draft system in the Vietnam War?

Conscientious objectors were required to undertake war work, such as working in weapons factories. There were around 17,000 COs in total, although almost 20 times as many men applied for exemption.

How did people avoid the draft in the Vietnam War?

Men living or working abroad could avoid the draft, but this option was only really available to the wealthy. Some 50,000 men went into hiding or left America illegally instead.

Why was the draft system unfair in the Vietnam War?

There were 3 main reasons the draft system was seen as unfair:

✅ Middle-class white men were often able to avoid the draft as they could afford to go to university or move abroad.

✅ Those with influential contacts could also dodge the draft.

✅ A disproportionate number of poor people, and those belonging to black and ethnic minorities, were therefore called up.

How many people refused to obey the draft for the Vietnam War?

9,000 men were prosecuted for refusing to be drafted.

What was the significance of the draft system in the Vietnam War?

The significance of the draft system to the Vietnam War *(p.43)* was its impact on the growing peace movement. Many people saw the system as unfair and engaged in protests.

DID YOU KNOW?

The average age of the American soldier in Vietnam was 19, compared to 26 in the Second World War. More than 35,000 of those who died were aged 21 or under.

THE TET OFFENSIVE

'The Tet Offensive failed because we underestimated our enemies and overestimated ourselves. We set goals which we realistically could not achieve.'
Vietcong general Tran Van Tra, writing in 1978

What happened during the Tet Offensive?

The Tet Offensive was a significant turning point in the Vietnam War *(p.43)*. The US government had told the public i was doing well in its fight against the Vietcong *(p.58)* and would soon be able to bring the war to an end. However, jus months later, the North Vietnamese and the Vietcong launched a series of major attacks in South Vietnam.

When did the Tet Offensive start?

The Tet Offensive started on 30th January, 1968. There was supposed to a ceasefire to allow for celebrations in honou Tet, a Vietnamese holiday celebrating the lunar new year.

Where did the Tet Offensive happen?

Hundreds of towns, cities and military bases were attacked during the Tet Offensive, along with General Westmoreland's base and the US embassy building, both in Saigon.

What was General Westmoreland's role in the Tet Offensive?

General Westmoreland was the commander of the US Army in Vietnam. He played a key role in the Tet Offensive as attacks caught him off guard. Months earlier he had presented the view to Congress that the war was going well. He 'We will prevail in Vietnam over the communist aggressor.'.

Why did the Tet Offensive happen?

The Tet Offensive had two aims:

- ☑ The Vietcong *(p.58)* and North Vietnamese government hoped it would win them support from the South Vietnam against the Americans, inspiring them to get rid of the current government and force the Americans from the country.
- ☑ They hoped a decisive victory against the Americans would attract media attention in the USA, weakening suppo from the war from its citizens.

What were the key events in the Tet Offensive?

There were a number of key events in the Tet Offensive:

- ☑ In the build up to the Tet Offensive the Vietcong *(p.58)* carried out smaller attacks, away from important cities, to d US troops. Around 50,000 American GIs were sent to defend these areas.
- ☑ On 30th January, 84,000 Vietcong *(p.58)* and North Vietnamese soldiers launched a number of attacks across Vietn
- ☑ The Americans were on the back foot to begin with. However, they recovered and quickly recaptured the towns, c and bases taken by the enemy during the attacks.
- ☑ The American embassy in Saigon was retaken by US paratroopers within hours.
- ☑ The communist forces were defeated in the Tet Offensive. 50,000 North Vietnamese troops and 10,000 Vietcong *(p.58)* soldiers were killed.

What were the failures of the Tet Offensive for the Vietcong?

Militarily, the Tet Offensive was a defeat for the Vietcong *(p.58)* and North Vietnam. They lost thousands of soldiers, a the USA re-took all cities, towns and bases.

What were the successes of the Tet Offensive for the Vietcong?

The Tet Offensive was both a political and psychological victory for a number of reasons.

- They had shown they could strike at any moment, and could take key cities and bases.
- The events were shown across US television, and the public saw the chaos and destruction. Americans now came to realise that, despite the clear advantage American military should have had, they were proving to be no match to the Vietcong's *(p.58)* guerrilla tactics.
- The American public started to turn against President Johnson *(p.102)* and the USA's involvement in the Vietnam War *(p.43)*. This was one of the Vietcong's *(p.58)* aims.

What were the results of the Tet Offensive?

The Tet Offensive was a huge turning point in the war, and had a number of consequences.

- The Americans began to question their involvement in Vietnam. They had been told, months before, that the end of the war was close. The Tet Offensive showed them that this was not true.
- The USA had spent vast sums of money, and many people had lost loved ones in the jungle of Vietnam, but the Vietcong *(p.58)* were able to strike a blow at the US embassy and showed no signs of letting up. It became clear to the US public that the war was not going to be over soon.
- In March 1968, President Johnson *(p.102)* told the US public that he would not be running in the next presidential election.
- In June 1968, General Westmoreland was replaced by General Creighton Abrams. It was clear that Johnson *(p.102)* was not happy with Westmoreland when he requested 200,000 more troops, and he turned down the request.
- The Tet Offensive had woken people up to the fact that the USA was now spending $30 billion a year fighting the Vietcong *(p.58)*, and 300 Americans were being killed every week in Vietnam.
- The Tet Offensive had also killed many civilians and destroyed many cities, further weakening support for the war.

> **DID YOU KNOW?**
>
> The Vietcong smuggled weapons and ammunition into Saigon for several months before the attacks.

THE MY LAI MASSACRE

'It was terrible. They were slaughtering villagers like so many sheep.'
Larry La Croix, American sergeant

What was the My Lai Massacre?

American troops went to the village of My Lai to search for Vietcong *(p.58)*. The American troops killed and abused over 500 women, children and old men.

When did the My Lai Massacre happen?

The My Lai Massacre happened on 16th March, 1968, not long after the Tet Offensive *(p.74)* began.

Where did the My Lai Massacre happen?

The massacre happened in a village called My Lai, in the Quang Ngai region of South Vietnam.

Who was involved in the My Lai Massacre?

Approximately 80 US soldiers from Charlie Company, a unit of the army's 11th Infantry Brigade, took part in the massacre.

Why did the My Lai Massacre happen?

There were 2 key reasons the massacre happened:

- ☑ Charlie Company was sent on a search and destroy *(p.70)* mission, following reports of a base of 200 Vietcong *(p. fighters in the area of My Lai. Reports suggested locals were giving them food, shelter and weapons, so Charlie Company was sent to burn all crops, livestock and food.
- ☑ Charlie Company had lost 5 soldiers in the Tet Offensive *(p.74)*. Although the unit had never directly fought the Vietcong *(p.58)*, it had experienced the organisation's guerrilla warfare while on patrol. It is thought the war had a psychological toll on the soldiers.

What were the key events in the My Lai Massacre?

There were a number of key events in the My Lai Massacre:

- ☑ At 7:30am on 16th March, 1968, 9 American helicopters landed near the village of My Lai. It was a Saturday, and was expected all the villagers would be at the market.
- ☑ Upon landing, the soldiers started shooting at any house they thought might contain Vietcong *(p.58)* soldiers.
- ☑ Grenades were used to destroy houses, crops and livestock.
- ☑ Some villagers tried to escape but the US forces shot or stabbed them. This was completely unwarranted; none o villagers had retaliated and most of those present were women and children.
- ☑ There were also several reports of Charlie Company troops torturing and raping civilians.
- ☑ No Vietcong *(p.58)* soldiers were found, and only a few weapons were recovered.
- ☑ Charlie Company returned to base and said 22 civilians were killed by accident, and the remaining dead were Vietcong *(p.58)*.

How was the My Lai Massacre covered up?

At first, Charlie Company received much recognition for its efforts. As the truth emerged, the government attempt cover up:

- ☑ The government announced the troops had killed 128 Vietcong *(p.58)* fighters and destroyed their base.
- ☑ However, some soldiers and local inhabitants reported what had really happened.
- ☑ The army attempted a cover-up, but one soldier, Ronald Ridenhour, made his eye-witness account public. He wr more than 30 letters to politicians and military officials, saying 'something rather dark and bloody' had happen My Lai a year earlier.
- ☑ General Westmoreland received one of Ridenhour's letters. Although he didn't believe it, he ordered an inquiry. army later admitted to 20 accidental civilian deaths.

What happened when the My Lai Massacre was investigated?

Two inquiries were held into the events of the My Lai Massacre, one by the government and the other by the army.

What did the government's investigation conclude about the My Lai Massacre?

The government investigation into the My Lai Massacre came to two main conclusions:

- ☑ It interviewed 398 witnesses and the weight of evidence indicated Charlie Company had massacred approximate 347 unarmed civilians.
- ☑ All those involved in the torture, rape, murder and cover up of the massacre should be punished.

What did the army's investigation into the My Lai Massacre conclude?

The army's investigation reported widespread failures and came to several conclusions:

- ☑ There were significant failures in the leadership and discipline of the soldiers.
- ☑ The soldiers were not experienced enough to carry out the roles they had been assigned to.

- ☑ The psychological trauma experienced by the men of Charlie Company created a desire for revenge against the Vietnamese.
- ☑ 25 men should be prosecuted for the massacre, either because of their participation or their involvement in the cover up.

How many were prosecuted because of their role in the My Lai Massacre?

Although the army said 25 men should be prosecuted, and some did face murder charges, only Lieutenant William Calley was prosecuted.

Who was Lieutenant Calley in the My Lai Massacre?

Lieutenant William Calley was one of the soldiers in charge of Charlie Company on the day of the massacre. He was responsible for the murder of 109 civilians at My Lai.

What was the role of Lieutenant Calley in the My Lai Massacre?

Calley played a leading role in the day's events. In accounts of what happened from other soldiers, Calley is reported to have said the following:

- ☑ In response to questions about a group of men, women and children gathered in the centre of the village by soldiers, he said: 'You know what I want you to do with them.'.
- ☑ On returning 10 minutes later and finding the group still there, he said: 'Haven't you got rid of them yet? I want them dead. Waste them.'.

What happened to Lieutenant Calley following his trial for the My Lai Massacre?

Lieutenant Calley was sentenced to life imprisonment. President Nixon *(p. 106)* received more than 5,000 telegrams in protest as many were outraged by the sentence, believing Calley was only following orders. In response, Calley was confined to an army base on President Nixon's orders and released after three and a half years.

What was the public's response to the My Lai Massacre?

Newspaper reports surfaced in November 1970 that claimed more than 500 civilians had been murdered in the massacre . On 5th December, pictures taken by an army photographer were shown on television, prompting a massive outcry.

What were the consequences of the My Lai Massacre?

The My Lai Massacre had 3 main consequences:

- ☑ It greatly strengthened the growing peace movement. People were repulsed by the atrocities committed by Charlie Company and questioned the morality of the USA's involvement in Vietnam.
- ☑ Due to the cover up of the massacre, people distrusted the government and the army. They did not believe they were being told the full truth about the war.
- ☑ The massacre led to further investigations and, in 1971, it was found over a third of US troops were addicted to drugs. It was clear morale was at an all-time low.

DID YOU KNOW?

Reports suggest some of Charlie Company emptied their guns into the ground as they did not want to participate in the massacre.

THE GROWING PEACE MOVEMENT

The peace movement saw an increase in opposition to the Vietnam War and played a major role in bringing it to an end.

What was the growing peace movement in the USA?

A poll in August 1965 showed that 61 per cent of the US population supported American troops in Vietnam. The publ bought into the importance of containing the spread of communism and both Johnson *(p.102)* and Kennedy *(p.103)* ha strong mandates to act against it. However, a peace movement against the war began to grow in the late 1960s.

When did the peace movement in the USA grow?

The anti-war movement began to grow significantly between 1965 and 1967, coinciding with the start of Operation Rolling Thunder *(p.65)* and the mass bombings of North Vietnam.

Where did the peace movement in the USA grow?

By 1967 there were protests all over America. A famous one in October 1967 saw over 100,000 demonstrators protes the Lincoln Memorial in Washington. It later continued outside the Pentagon, where there were violent clashes betv protesters and soldiers.

Why did the peace movement in the USA grow?

There were a number of reasons the peace movement grew in the USA:

- ☑ Some protestors questioned the morality of America's involvement.
- ☑ The broadcast of images from the war on television had an impact on people's views.
- ☑ Martin Luther King, the civil rights leader, had an impact on people's views.
- ☑ There was a lack of progress in President Johnson's 'Great Society' policies.
- ☑ The war was costing a lot, both financially and in terms of lives lost.
- ☑ The draft system *(p.72)* increased people's opposition to the war.

Why did questions over the morality of America's involvement in Vietnam cause a growth in the peace movement in the USA?

People questioned the morality of America's tactics in Vietnam and asked why America was involved in the affairs o another country on a different continent. America was not simply helping South Vietnam defend itself; it had attack North Vietnam. Many saw this as the action of an aggressor.

What was broadcast on television about the Vietnam War, leading to a growth in the peace movem in the USA?

Day after day, American television showed the reality of the Vietnam War *(p.43)*. People saw a lot of disturbing image

- ☑ They saw villages being blown up.
- ☑ They saw the jungle being napalmed.
- ☑ They heard reports of massacres where civilians were tortured, raped and murdered, such as at My Lai.
- ☑ They heard of young American soldiers being injured or killed by the barbaric Vietcong *(p.58)* booby traps.
- ☑ They saw mounting numbers of body bags arriving home from the war.

Why did the portrayal of the war on television cause a growth in the peace movement in the USA?

The television images of the Vietnam War *(p.43)* shocked people, and added weight to questions over the morality of America's involvement in the war. People did not think it was in America's interests to continue.

Why did the role of Martin Luther King cause a growth in the peace movement across the USA?

The role of Martin Luther King led to a growth in the peace movement in the USA for a number of reasons:

☑ He spoke out about inequalities in the recruitment of troops. Between 1966 and 1969, 246,000 men were recruited to fight in Vietnam; 41 per cent were black Americans, yet they only made up 11 per cent of America's population. By 1968, black Americans made up 12 per cent of the army, but 50 per cent of men serving on the frontline.

☑ King argued the war was immoral, saying the money spent on fighting in Vietnam should go towards domestic programmes to improve the lives of Americans.

Why did pressure on President Johnson to fulfil his election promise of a 'Great Society' lead to a growth in the peace movement?

In 1964, Johnson *(p. 102)* had campaigned on a programme of improving housing, education, healthcare and employment - the 'Great Society'. People became frustrated as there was little progress, yet the costs of the war were spiralling. Money earmarked for raising living standards was used to fund the war instead.

Why did the cost of the war lead to a growth in the peace movement?

The cost of the war led to a growth in the peace movement for 3 main reasons:

☑ The war was a huge financial burden on the USA. By 1967 it cost $30 billion per year. This meant other important areas of the economy, such as domestic reform, were neglected.

☑ Families across America were paying a high price in terms of the loved ones they lost. By the end of 1967 there were 500,000 US soldiers in Vietnam, and 40,000 more sent each month. 15,000 troops had lost their lives and 110,000 were wounded.

☑ For those soldiers who were injured, the war cost them their quality of life. Many lost limbs and were wheelchair-bound for the rest of their lives. Many suffered from post-traumatic stress.

Why did the draft lead to a growth in the peace movement?

Many young men recruited to fight in Vietnam as a result of the draft resented being forced to fight a war they did not agree with.

How did people protest as the peace movement grew in the USA?

As the peace movement grew people protested in a number of ways:

☑ A group of university students established 'Students for Democratic Society' and protested through 'teach ins'. They held debates and lectures, and sang songs against the war.

☑ In October 1967, 100,000 people protested at the Lincoln Memorial in Washington.

☑ Veterans of the war established 'Vietnam Veterans Against the War'. They protested by throwing away the medals they had received.

☑ Many young men called up by the draft burned their draft cards very publicly.

☑ Student protests involved over 40,000 students chanting 'Hey, hey, LBJ *(p. 102)*! How many kids did you kill today?', aimed as a criticism at President Johnson. Many people believed he had the blood of both US soldiers and Vietnamese civilians on his hands.

What was the impact of the growing peace movement on the war in Vietnam?

The growing peace movement in the USA had a significant impact on the war.

☑ The personal criticism upset Johnson *(p. 102)*, so much so he declared that he would not run in the next presidential election in 1968.

☑ The peace movement was a significant factor in the USA's withdrawal from Vietnam in the 1970s, under President Nixon *(p. 106)*.

NIXON'S WAR

Richard Nixon was the president who ended the Vietnam War - although for a while, it appeared he was simply widening its scope.

What was Richard Nixon's involvement in the Vietnam War?

Nixon took office at a time when America had made little progress in fighting the Vietcong *(p.58)* or containing communism in the region. Growing demands for peace, and the realisation the US couldn't win, led Nixon to promi the war would end with an 'honourable peace' US troops brought home.

What were Richard Nixon's views on America's involvement in Vietnam?

Nixon believed the USA should withdraw from Vietnam. He understood clearly that the conflict couldn't be won wi traditional military tactics; neither could he engage in nuclear warfare as this would provoke China and the USSR a threaten a nuclear apocalypse. However, he had not abandoned the USA's commitment to contain communism.

What influenced Richard Nixon's views on America's involvement in Vietnam?

There were several key influences on Nixon's strategy for Vietnam:

- ☑ Public trust in the government was low, so he had to ensure whatever course of action he took was supported by public.
- ☑ Nixon had a double burden. He knew he had to withdraw US troops from Vietnam but, like his predecessors, he not want to be known as the president who lost South Vietnam to communism.
- ☑ He had served as vice-president to Eisenhower and shared his views on the importance of containment. Nixon v operating in the context of the Cold War *(p.16)*.

What were the key events in Richard Nixon's involvement in Vietnam?

There were a number of key events in Nixon's involvement in Vietnam:

- ☑ On 3rd November, 1969, he announced his policy of Vietnamisation *(p.81)*.
- ☑ By the end of 1969, 85,000 of the 540,000 US soldiers in Vietnam had been withdrawn.
- ☑ In March 1969, Nixon authorised the bombing of Cambodia. This was initially kept secret, but was later seen as a widening of the war.
- ☑ In April 1970, he authorised an invasion of Cambodia by the US Army.
- ☑ In May 1970, students protested at the Kent State *(p.86)* University in Ohio - one of the most famous demonstratic against the war.
- ☑ In May 1970, Nixon declared 150,000 more troops were needed. This led to huge demonstrations throughout the USA.
- ☑ In February 1971, US forces launched an attack on North Vietnamese soldiers in Laos.
- ☑ In the spring of 1972, the North Vietnamese attacked South Vietnam.

- [x] As part of a wider policy of détente (the easing of tensions between countries), the USA entered discussions with the USSR regarding arms limitations. Nixon also requested that the USSR put pressure on the North Vietnamese to end the war.
- [x] Nixon was the first US president to be invited to communist China. During his visit, in February 1972, he also asked China to put pressure on North Vietnam to end the conflict.
- [x] In October 1972, North Vietnam proposed an 'in place' ceasefire.
- [x] On 27th January, 1973, the Paris Peace Accord (p.94) was signed and brought an end to the conflict.
- [x] In March 1973, the last US soldiers left Vietnam.

What was the significance of Richard Nixon's involvement in the Vietnam War?

Nixon's involvement in the Vietnam War (p.43) was significant as, under his leadership, the conflict came to an end. While it did appear for some time this might not happen - as there was an expansion of the war during his presidency - he fulfilled his commitment to bring US troops home.

DID YOU KNOW?

Despite Nixon's promises to withdraw US troops from Vietnam after he took office in 1969, in April the number of US soldiers in Vietnam reached an all-time high of 543,000.

VIETNAMISATION

'I ordered first a substantial increase in the training and equipment of South Vietnamese forces.'
Richard Nixon, 1969

What was Vietnamisation?

Vietnamisation was a US policy to end American involvement in Vietnam by developing the South Vietnamese army.

When was the policy of Vietnamisation introduced?

The policy of Vietnamisation was officially announced on 3rd November, 1969. By spring 1972, when US forces attacked Laos, it was evident the policy was failing.

Who was involved in the policy of Vietnamisation?

The policy of Vietnamisation was the idea of President Nixon (p.106), who implemented it during his time in office.

What were the aims of the policy of Vietnamisation?

The policy of Vietnamisation had a number of aims:

- [x] It aimed to make the ARVN self-sufficient, so it could defend South Vietnam without US support.
- [x] This, in turn, would enable Nixon to withdraw US troops from Vietnam.

Why was the policy of Vietnamisation introduced?

The policy of Vietnamisation was introduced for a number of reasons:

- [x] Nixon was realistic about the unlikelihood of victory in Vietnam, and knew he had to bring an end to the war.
- [x] Nixon could not use nuclear weapons to do this, so he had to find another way.
- [x] Nixon was anti-communist and did not want South Vietnam to fall to communism.

- ☑ Nixon believed the South Vietnamese should take responsibility for their own defence.
- ☑ Nixon needed to find a practical solution to the war quickly, as a poll in early 1969 showed 56 per cent of America thought US involvement in Vietnam was wrong.

What problems did President Nixon face when implementing the policy of Vietnamisation?

At the same time as Nixon implemented Vietnamisation, with the intention of withdrawing US troops, he was also extending the war into into Cambodia and Laos. For this, he needed more soldiers. In April 1970 he announced 100,0 more troops were needed, prompting widespread demonstrations across the USA.

How did the policy of Vietnamisation work?

There were a number of aspects to the policy of Vietnamisation:

- ☑ The USA was to provide training and equipment for the expansion of the ARVN.
- ☑ Local villagers would be recruited as civilian militia, in charge of securing rural areas.
- ☑ The ARVN would take a more direct role in seeking out the Vietcong (p. 58). Since 1965 they had taken a back seat t US.
- ☑ Between 1968 and 1971, the ARVN was increased from 393,000 to 532,000 troops.
- ☑ As the ARVN became more self-sufficient, US troops would be withdrawn from Vietnam. The first notable depar was on 7th July, 1969.
- ☑ By the beginning of 1970 the ARNV had been equipped with $4 billion worth of military supplies, including rifle artillery, munitions, and helicopters.
- ☑ ARNV officers had received specialised training in command, military strategy, and counter-insurgency warfare

Was the policy of Vietnamisation successful?

The policy of Vietnamisation made South Vietnam one of the most militarised countries in Asia, and half the South Vietnamese population had been recruited. But it was a failure.

Why did Vietnamisation fail?

Vietnamisation failed for a number of reasons.

- ☑ There was a poor harvest in 1972.
- ☑ There was corruption and theft.
- ☑ The US did not provide enough funding.
- ☑ The ARVN soldiers were not adequately trained.
- ☑ The South Vietnamese government was very unpopular.
- ☑ The ARVN was militarily weak and corrupt.
- ☑ South Vietnam was economically weak.

How did corruption cause Vietnamisation to fail?

The stealing of supplies and equipment was common. Officers regularly took bribes, which allowed thieves to steal goods. This cost the US Army millions of dollars in lost equipment, and meant that troops were not adequately suppl This made winning the war harder.

How did funding cause the failure of Vietnamisation?

The amount of funding available was restricted by the US Congress. This limited the capability and options available the US military.

How did the inadequate training of the ARVN troops lead to the failure of the policy of Vietnamisation?

The training of ARVN troops was rushed. Instructions for equipment use and operation were given in English, which the Vietnamese could not understand. Without US support, the ARVN was unable to continue fighting.

How did the unpopularity of the South Vietnamese government lead to the failure of the policy of Vietnamisation?

The South Vietnamese people disliked their own government. It was weak and divided, and they saw it as a puppet of a US administration that was also corrupt. It could not survive without billions of dollars of aid provided by America.

How did the military weaknesses and the corruption of the ARNV lead to the failure of the policy of Vietnamisation?

American had thrown significant funding at the ARVN, but they couldn't change the fact it was a much divided organisation, riddled with corruption and incompetence. Even though the US had provided training, its leaders were incapable of commanding the respect of their men, and did not have the morale needed to combat the Vietcong *(p.58)*.

How did the economic weaknesses of South Vietnam lead to the failure of the policy of Vietnamisation?

The USA had been propping up the South Vietnamese government since the 1950s, and it had become dependent on American funding. At the same time, the US was looking to gradually withdraw funding, while the USSR and China were sending significant funds to the government in North Vietnam.

DID YOU KNOW?

There were many critics of the policy of Vietnamisation. A British cartoon in May 1972 had the caption: 'If this boy of yours is real, how come we gotta wind him up all the time?' The message was that the newly trained ARVN troops lacked motivation to fight on their own.

RELATIONS WITH THE USSR AND CHINA IN THE 1970S

President Nixon made great efforts to improve relations with the USSR and China - hoping they would help to end the Vietnam War.

What was America's relationship with China and the USSR like under Nixon?

America's relationship with China and the USSR under Nixon was far less hostile than it had been in previous years.

Why was there an improvement in America's relationship with China and the USSR under Nixon?

There were a number of reasons for the improvement:

- ☑ The USA and the USSR were pursuing the policy of détente. This was a relaxing of tensions between the two sides.
- ☑ The USA and USSR wanted to reduce tensions because the arms race - the build up of nuclear weapons - was becoming a huge economic burden for both sides.
- ☑ Nixon was under huge pressure to bring an end to the war in Vietnam, and this would be less challenging if he could improve relations with China and the USSR.
- ☑ The Sino-Soviet split (a souring between China and the USSR) paved the way for the USA and China to rebuild relations.

What were the results of America's improved relationship with China and the USSR under Nixon

America's improved relationship with China and the USSR had a number of results:

- ☑ Improved relations with China led to a symbolic visit to the country by Nixon in February 1972.
- ☑ Nixon also made a historic trip to the USSR, to meet leader Leonid Brezhnev, in May 1972. Photos of Nixon and Brezhnev shaking hands made the front pages of media across the world.
- ☑ The USA dropped its objections to China becoming a member of the United Nations *(p.25)*.
- ☑ Nixon used the improved relations as an opportunity to persuade China and the USSR to pressure North Vietnam into ending the war.

DID YOU KNOW?

A group of table tennis (ping pong) players became the first Americans to visit communist China in April 1971. The trip is often praised for reviving diplomatic relations between the two countries, which hadn't been in contact for 22 years, and became known as 'ping pong diplomacy'. Nixon visited China a year later.

THE WIDENING OF THE WAR INTO CAMBODIA AND LAOS

The Vietnam War spread into neighbouring countries.

What was the widening of the Vietnam War?

Despite President Nixon *(p.106)* committing to the withdrawal of US troops from Vietnam in 1969, when he announced the policy of Vietnamisation *(p.81)*, thousands more were sent to fight in the conflict as it expanded into neighbouring countries.

Where was the Vietnam War widened to?

The Vietnam War *(p.43)* was widened to Cambodia, on the western border of South Vietnam, and to Laos, on the western border of North Vietnam.

When was the Vietnam War widened to Cambodia and Laos?

Nixon sanctioned a bombing campaign on Cambodia in March 1969, and an attack on Laos in early 1971.

 Why was the Vietnam War widened to Cambodia and Laos?

The Vietnam War *(p.43)* was widened to Cambodia and Laos in an attempt to weaken the Vietcong *(p.58)*. The Ho Chi Minh Trail *(p.59)* that supplied the Vietcong ran through both countries, and US forces also wanted to destroy Vietcong bases positioned just across the border in Cambodia.

 What happened when the Vietnam War was widened to Cambodia?

The following happened when the war stretched into Cambodia:

- ☑ In March 1969, US air forces were authorised to carry out a bombing campaign targeting the Ho Chi Minh Trail *(p.59)* and Vietcong *(p.58)* bases.
- ☑ The bombing was kept secret as it was at odds with Nixon's policy of withdrawal and he wanted to avoid international condemnation.
- ☑ When the bombing campaign failed to achieve its objectives, a ground invasion of Cambodia was launched. Nixon announced a need for 150,000 more troops, which was met by a wave of protests.

✅ The US troops alienated the local population in Cambodia. A communist group called the Khmer Rouge saw its membership increase rapidly as a result, as the local peasants were convinced the USA planned to take over.

What happened when the Vietnam War was widened to Laos?

The following happened when the war widened into Laos:

✅ After extensive training under Nixon's policy of Vietnamisation *(p.81)*, the ARVN was sent to carry out an attack on Ho Chi Minh's *(p.105)* army in Laos.

✅ The ARVN was quickly pushed back into Vietnam.

✅ The ARVN's actions provoked a retaliatory attack on South Vietnam by the North Vietnamese army in the spring of 1972.

✅ The ARVN's attacks led to the Pathet Lao, a communist organisation in Laos, becoming more popular with the locals. By 1973, it controlled much of Laos.

What were the consequences of widening the Vietnam War to Cambodia and Laos?

The widening of the war in Cambodia and Laos had a number of consequences:

✅ The attacks further increased the need for US troops, which was unpopular with the American people.

✅ The attacks led to further protests across America.

✅ North Vietnamese troops attacked South Vietnam.

✅ It highlighted the failures of the policy of Vietnamisation *(p.81)*.

DID YOU KNOW?

The bombings of Cambodia were kept secret as Nixon knew they would be met with international condemnation.

THE STUDENT MOVEMENT AGAINST THE VIETNAM WAR

'Hell no, we won't go.'
A popular student slogan against the war

What was the student movement?

The student movement was a left-wing crusade which wanted to transform American society. It focused on perceived social, political and economic injustices of the time.

When did the student movement develop?

The student movement began to gain momentum at the end of the 1960s and in the early 1970s.

Why did the student movement develop?

There were 4 key reasons the student movement developed:

✅ Students wanted a greater say in their education at college and university.

✅ Students wanted a form of participatory democracy in which people had more say in politics and more control over decisions made by the government.

✅ Students wanted to end racism and fight for civil rights.

✅ Students were against the Vietnam War *(p.43)*.

Why did the student movement oppose the Vietnam War?

The student movement against the Vietnam War *(p.43)* grew for 8 key reasons:

- Media coverage turned people against the war.
- 12 per cent of soldiers that fought in the war ended up either dead or seriously injured. The number of amputatio was approximately 300 per cent higher than in the Second World War.
- The average age of an American GI killed in Vietnam was 23.
- 2,000,000 men were forced to fight in Vietnam between 1964 and 1972 as a result of the draft.
- Leading figures like Martin Luther King and Muhammad Ali highlighted issues of racial inequality in the US for
- People did not like the corruption and brutality of the South Vietnamese government as it was undemocratic.
- Even politicians began to question the war, which was distracting the government from pressing domestic issues education and healthcare.
- The USA was losing against the Vietcong *(p.58)*. Events like the Tet Offensive *(p.74)* and My Lai Massacre *(p.75)* brou this home to the American people.

 How did students and hippies protest against the war in Vietnam as part of the student movement

Examples of protests and demonstrations included:

- 500,000 people came together in Washington on 15th November, 1969, to listen to speeches and songs about end the war. It was the biggest anti-war protest in US history.
- Hippies protested by rejecting the traditional American way of life. Not working or going to school, growing hair long and taking illegal drugs was seen as a rejection of government and authority.
- Student protests became increasingly violent and there were many clashes with police.
- In August 1970, at the University of Wisconsin-Madison in Wisconsin, a bomb was detonated by student proteste One person was killed and several others injured.
- In May 1970, there were protests at the Kent State *(p.86)* University which resulted in the deaths of 4 students.

 What was the significance of the student movement to the Vietnam War?

The student movement was significant as it was a key factor in the eventual withdrawal of US forces from Vietnam.

DID YOU KNOW?

The student movement had a huge effect on popular culture. Artists like John Lennon and Bob Dylan had big hits with anti-war songs.

THE KENT STATE UNIVERSITY SHOOTINGS

'Remember Kent State, May 4, 1970: An iconic moment for a generation... a coming of conscience for a country.'
Rita Dragonette

 What was the Kent State Protest?

The Kent State Protest, or Kent State shootings, involved the shooting and killing of unarmed university students wh were protesting against the Vietnam War *(p.43)*.

When did the Kent State University protest shootings happen?

The Kent State protest occurred between 1st and 4th May, 1970. The shootings took place on the final day.

Where did the Kent State Shootings happen?

The shootings happened at Kent State University in the state of Ohio.

Why did the Kent State University protest shootings happen?

There were 2 main reasons for the shootings:

☑ Protestors were demonstrating at the university against the Vietnam War *(p.43)*. This was prompted by Nixon's announcement of the invasion of Cambodia and the need for 150,000 more US troops.

☑ The Ohio state governor had sent in the National Guard to stop the demonstrations that had taken place all weekend. On the Monday, the protests turned violent and events escalated to the shootings.

What were the key events in the Kent State University protest shootings?

There were 6 key events in the Kent State University protest shootings:

☑ President Nixon *(p.106)* announced to the American public that US forces had invaded Cambodia on 30th April, 1970.

☑ Protests across America took place the next day at many colleges and universities, including Kent State University.

☑ Protests continued over the weekend, often escalating to clashes between protesters and police. Windows were smashed and police cars vandalised.

☑ With further protests planned for Monday, 4th May, amid fears of continued violence, 1,000 National Guardsmen were sent to stop them.

☑ Just after midday, violence erupted. Students threw rocks and the National Guardsmen responded with tear gas.

☑ In the chaos, at 12.24pm, some of the National Guardsmen started shooting at the protesters. 4 students, including one called Jeffrey Miller, were killed and a further 9 were injured.

What happened to the National Guardsmen that had carried out the shootings at the Kent State University protest?

The government investigated the shootings and a report stated that the guardsmen's actions were "unnecessary, unwarranted, and inexcusable". 8 of them were arrested but there was not enough evidence to prosecute.

Why were the shootings at the Kent State Protest controversial?

The students killed in the Kent State shootings were white and middle class, which was why there was such public outrage. When two black students were shot and 12 injured during an anti-war protest at Jackson State University, there was very little publicity or reaction.

What was significant about the shootings at the Kent State University protest?

The shootings were significant as it strengthened the anti-war movement further and led to increased calls for America to withdraw from Vietnam.

DID YOU KNOW?

In the aftermath of the shootings Nixon met with student demonstrations and famously said: 'I know that probably most of you think I'm an SOB.'

THE ROLE OF THE MEDIA AND TV IN INFLUENCING PUBLI OPINION ABOUT THE VIETNAM WAR

'Television brought the brutality of war into the comfort of the living room. Vietnam was lost in the living rooms of America - not on the battlefields of Vietnam.'
Marshall McLuhan

What media coverage was there of the Vietnam War?

US media coverage continued to expand as the war continued. In 1964 there were fewer than 10 journalists in Vietn but by 1968 there were over 600. Television also played a part in bringing the war into American homes.

What are some examples of media coverage of the Vietnam War?

Examples of media coverage of the Vietnam War *(p.43)* included:

- ☑ The Tet Offensive *(p.74)* in January 1968. Coverage showed Vietnamese civilians being killed and ancient monum destroyed.
- ☑ In February 1968 there were news stories of General Nguyen Ngoc Loan's execution of a Vietcong *(p.58)* fighter.
- ☑ In November 1969 the media broke the truth about the My Lai Massacre *(p.75)*.

Why was there an increase in media coverage of the Vietnam War?

Media coverage of the Vietnam War *(p.43)* increased for the following reasons:

- ☑ To begin with, there were few troops in Vietnam. In 1960 there were only 900 'military advisers', and no reporte
- ☑ This changed in 1960 when local Vietnamese people were killed in an attack against Diem *(p.100)*, the South Vietnamese president. Many journalists travelled to Vietnam to report on the event.
- ☑ As US involvement in the war increased, so too did the number of journalists covering the conflict. By 1965 there were 400 foreign news reporters in Vietnam - an increase of 900 per cent on 1964.
- ☑ Since the Second World War, there had been a significant increase in the number of Americans who owned a television. In 1948, just 1 per cent of American households had a television; by 1961, this had risen to 93 per cent.
- ☑ Journalists were better equipped to report the news with ground-breaking technology such as video cameras an voice recorders. It helped reporters capture the reality of the war and broadcast it to America and the world.
- ☑ There was no censorship on coverage of the Vietnam War *(p.43)*. The Second World War and Korean War *(p.22)* ha been filmed by military cameramen, but Vietnam was caught on film by by independent television networks.

What was the early media coverage of the Vietnam War like?

Early coverage of events in Vietnam mostly included positive reporting on the courage of American soldiers and th technology used in weaponry. In the context of the Cold War *(p.16)*, it portrayed the USA as the 'goodies', fighting the communist 'baddies' of North Vietnam.

What were the 'five o'clock follies' in media coverage of the Vietnam War?

As the war intensified in the mid 1960s, US forces met with journalists covering the conflict daily at 5:00pm. The journalists would jeer and mock the military officials as they felt the truth was being hidden about the extent of fail of the US Army in Vietnam. These meetings became known as the 'five o'clock follies' as they were seen as useless.

What was the significance of media coverage of the Tet Offensive in the Vietnam War?

The TV media coverage of the Tet Offensive *(p.74)* was significant for the following reasons:

- ☑ The coverage resulted in a change in how the war was reported and how the public perceived the conflict.
- ☑ For many months officials had assured the public that they were winning the war, however the TV media covera the Tet Offensive *(p.74)* contradicted this.
- ☑ TV reports of the Tet Offensive *(p.74)* showed the fall of the US embassy of Saigon - a symbolic defeat in the eyes c Americans (although the US eventually won it back).

✅ Viewers saw the brutality of the war, and after the Tet Offensive *(p.74)* many people did not trust what they were being told.

How did media coverage expose the government's lies to the public about the Vietnam War?

People lost faith when they realised the government was not being completely honest about what was happening in Vietnam. For example, the US government claimed victory in the Tet Offensive *(p.74)*, but CBS journalist Walter Cronkite *(p.100)* reported the reality and showed that it was a stalemate.

What was the 'credibility gap' on television during the Vietnam War?

The 'credibility gap' was the term used to describe the difference between what the US government said was happening, and what people saw happening on TV.

What was the significance of Walter Cronkite's role in media coverage of the Vietnam War?

The role of Walter Cronkite *(p.100)* was significant for the following reasons:

✅ Walter Cronkite *(p.100)* was a famous news broadcaster, seen as one of the 'most trusted men in America'. His coverage of the war played a huge role in the peace movement.

✅ In one of his news broadcasts for CBS, in February 1967, he said: 'It seems now more certain than ever, that the bloody experience of Vietnam is to end a stalemate… it is increasingly clear to the only rational way out then will be to negotiate.'.

✅ Cronkite was so influential that President Johnson *(p.102)* once said to an advisor: 'If I have lost Cronkite, I've lost this country.'.

✅ When Walter Cronkite *(p.100)* made his famous statement on the Tet Offensive *(p.74)* in 1968, it was considered a turning point in the media and public attitude, and the beginning of the fading of support for the war.

What was the significance of media coverage of the My Lai Massacre in the Vietnam War?

Coverage of the My Lai Massacre *(p.75)* in March 1968, was significant because it damaged the reputation of the US forces. Americans were shocked and appalled about both the reports of their soldiers murdering innocent people but also the fact that the army and government had tried to cover it up.

What was the impact of media coverage of the Vietnam War?

The TV media coverage of the Vietnam War *(p.43)* had the following impacts:

✅ It led to a lack of trust in the US Army and the government. When the New York Times published leaked reports of American actions in Vietnam in June 1971 that were supposed to be secret many felt they had been lied to about the war.

✅ The media coverage influenced public opinion. When the names and faces of over 200 US soldiers were published during a week of fighting in 1969, people became angry about fighting a distant war.

✅ As more and more stories were published of soldiers and civilians dying and the brutality of the war, this affected the morale and behaviour in the US forces.

✅ The failure of US tactics in Vietnam was widely published and clear for Americans to see on the television and this led to more people questioning the point of the war and if the USA could win.

✅ The anti-war movement was further strengthened by the TV media coverage of the conflict.

DID YOU KNOW?

By 1960 it is estimated 60 per cent of Americans got their news from television.

THE IMPACT OF THE WATERGATE SCANDAL ON THE VIETNAM WAR

Watergate was considered the biggest constitutional crisis in American history.

What was Watergate?

Watergate was a political scandal involving President Richard Nixon *(p.106)*, leading to his resignation in 1974.

When did the Watergate scandal happen?

The events of Watergate took place between 1971 and 1974. The burglary at the centre of the scandal happened on 17t. June, 1972. Details were first published in the media during that month, and eventually it led to Nixon's resignation 9th August, 1974.

Who was involved with the Watergate scandal?

There were 4 main individuals or groups involved in Watergate:

- ☑ President Richard Nixon *(p.106)*, who lied about interfering with the investigation.
- ☑ The Committee to Re-elect the President, or CREEP.
- ☑ Washington Post journalists Carl Bernstein and Bob Woodward, who investigated the events.
- ☑ The FBI, who investigated what happened.

How was Nixon involved in Watergate?

President Richard Nixon *(p.106)* was involved in the Watergate scandal in 5 main ways:

- ☑ CREEP, or the Committee to Re-elect the President, was created to raise money for his 1972 re-election campaign committed crimes by spying on his opponents, the Democrats.
- ☑ He provided funds for CREEP that enabled its members to spy. Some of the money was used to fund a break-in at National Democratic Committee offices.
- ☑ He blocked the initial investigation, attempted to cover up the wrongdoing, and interfered with the FBI's investigation.
- ☑ He initially refused to hand over tapes of conversations held in the Oval Office to the FBI which contained eviden. relevant to their investigation.
- ☑ He resigned as president on 9th August, 1974, before he could be impeached for his involvement in the scandal.

What was the impact of the Watergate scandal on the Vietnam War?

The scandal hugely eroded the public's trust in American politics and people began to wonder how many cover-ups there were in the Vietnam War *(p.43)*. People simply did not trust what they were being told and the anti-war movem. was further strengthened.

DID YOU KNOW?

As the Watergate scandal became public it was discovered there were illegal wiretaps and recordings of conversations. Nixon's tapes proved his illegal activities and those of his staff.

Quizzes, amazing exam preparation tools and more at GCSEHistory.com

POLITICAL OPPOSITION TO THE WAR

'I speak for those whose land is being laid waste, whose homes are being destroyed, whose culture is being subverted. I speak for the poor of America who are paying the double price of smashed hopes at home… I speak as a citizen of the world, for the world, as it stands aghast at the path we have taken.'
Dr Martin Luther King, 1967

What political opposition was there to the Vietnam War?

Politicians began to oppose the war for a number of reasons, as they responded to public sentiment. They demonstrated their opposition in Congress and other governing institutions, as well as publicly.

What were the reasons for political opposition to the Vietnam War?

Politicians opposed the war for 5 main reasons:

- ☑ It seemed unwinnable. Events like the Tet Offensive *(p.74)* demonstrated the strength of the Vietcong *(p.58)*, and the invasion of Laos proved the policy of Vietnamisation *(p.81)* was not working.

- ☑ The cost was extremely high. It is estimated the war cost the US government $170 billion - around $1 trillion in today's money. The financial burden meant domestic spending programmes on things like education and healthcare were neglected.

- ☑ It risked destroying international relations. Many nations, including the United Kingdom which had a 'special relationship' with the USA, distanced themselves from the Vietnam War *(p.43)*. The UK did not join the war as it felt it was hypocritical to fight against a nation battling for independence.

- ☑ The US opposition party, the Democrats, saw opposing the war as a way to criticise the administration and gain power.

- ☑ Media coverage, particularly on television, brought home the brutality of war to politicians and the public alike.

What international political opposition was there to the Vietnam War?

The USA was condemned by many countries for incidents such as the My Lai Massacre *(p.75)* and its use of chemical weapons.

How did the media affect the political opposition to the Vietnam War?

The media coverage of events such as the My Lai Massacre *(p.75)* and Kent State *(p.86)* shootings, along with photographs of the horrific effects of Agent Orange and napalm, sparked shock and outrage worldwide. Some politicians were embarrassed to be American.

What was the significance of the political opposition to the Vietnam War.

The political opposition to the Vietnam War *(p.43)* was significant because it contributed to the reasons for US withdrawal from Vietnam *(p.92)*. The US government came under increasing pressure from both the public and leading politicians to bring US troops home from Vietnam.

DID YOU KNOW?

Even politicians who supported the war to begin with, like Robert McNamara, eventually turned against American involvement.

THE EASTER OFFENSIVE

'The bastards have never been bombed like they're going to be bombed this time.'
President Nixon in reaction to the Easter Offensive in 1972

What was the North Vietnam Easter Offensive?

North Vietnam launched a surprise attack against the south in March 1972.

What happened during North Vietnam's Easter Offensive?

Around 120,000 troops from North Vietnam and the Vietcong *(p.58)* attacked three bases in South Vietnam. The South Vietnamese ARVN, with air support from the USA, managed to repel the attack.

What did the USA do during the North Vietnam bombing offensive?

In April 1972, the USA retaliated with Operation Linebacker. This involved heavy bombing of North Vietnam, including the cities of Hanoi and Haiphong. They also blocked Chinese and Soviet ships from entering North Vietnamese waters.

What was the outcome of the North Vietnam bombing offensive?

The USA destroyed the majority of North Vietnam's war industry and supply routes. Most of its radio and communication networks were also demolished. China and the USSR started to encourage the north to negotiate for peace.

DID YOU KNOW?

The Easter Offensive is sometimes known as the 'Red Fiery Summer'.

THE US WITHDRAWAL

'The US government became involved in Vietnam slowly. Each step of the way, for more than 20 years, policymakers debated options, considered alternatives, and ultimately chose deeper involvement. By mid-1965, a series of incremental steps led to US ground troops facing combat in Vietnam. By 1968 the war had become a quagmire with no clear road to victory.'
David R Farber

What was the US withdrawal from Vietnam?

Nixon had been elected as president on a promise to withdraw America from Vietnam and to secure an 'honourable peace'. During his presidency he worked to bring all US soldiers home from the conflict and end the war in Vietnam.

When was the US withdrawal from Vietnam?

Nixon began working on the process of withdrawal from January 1969 and the last American soldiers left the region in March 1973.

Why did the US withdraw from Vietnam?

There were a number of reasons the USA withdrew from Vietnam, including:

- ✅ The Americans realised the war was unwinnable. Their tactics had failed against the guerrilla warfare of the Viet (p.58).
- ✅ The morale of American soldiers in Vietnam was incredibly low, making it difficult to continue fighting.

✅ The economic cost of the war was proving too high. By the late 1960s it was costing $30 million a year, to the detriment of domestic programmes such as improving education and healthcare.

✅ When the conflict began the American people bought into the idea of saving South Vietnam from communism. However, by the end of the 1960s, they did not believe in the war any more. They felt it was not the USA's business, and money should not be spent on it while people suffered at home.

✅ Opposition to the war was reaching breaking point with incidents like the Kent State (p.86) University shootings. Political opposition was also increasing and trust in the government was at an all-time low.

✅ The role of the media hugely influenced public opinion about the war and was largely negative about America's involvement in Vietnam.

✅ The American people felt the war was immoral. Media coverage meant they witnessed the atrocities being committed in Vietnam by US forces, and they believed the killing of innocent people was wrong.

What was Nixon's approach to the US withdrawal from Vietnam?

Nixon's approach to the US withdrawal from Vietnam included the following:

✅ A key policy was Vietnamisation (p.81), introduced in 1969. The idea was for that training from US forces would enable the South Vietnamese army (ARVN) to become self-sufficient in fighting the Vietcong (p.58), meaning Nixon could bring American troops home.

✅ He used his political experience to encourage the South Vietnamese government to reach a compromise with North Vietnam. He also used improved relationships with the USSR and China to persuade them to pressure Ho Chi Minh (p.105) to bring an end to the war.

✅ He used his National Security Adviser, a particularly talented politician called Henry Kissinger (p.104), to try and negotiate a ceasefire with North Vietnam.

✅ He increased the bombing of North Vietnam and expanded the targets to include Vietcong (p.58) supply routes in Cambodia and Laos. He hoped this would force Ho Chi Minh (p.105) to the negotiating table and bring an end to the war.

What were the key events in the US withdrawal from Vietnam?

The key events in the US withdrawal from Vietnam included the following:

✅ In January 1969, Nixon sent Henry Cabot Lodge to Paris to begin peace talks with the North Vietnamese government representative, Le Duc.

✅ In March 1969, US forces carried out a bombing campaign in Cambodia to destroy the Ho Chi Minh trail (p.59) and cut off the Vietcong (p.58) from South Vietnam.

✅ 25,000 troops were withdrawn from Vietnam in June 1969 as part of the policy of Vietnamisation (p.81).

✅ In August 1969, Henry Kissinger (p.104) conducted secret talks with Le Duc. It was thought if the talks were kept secret, people could talk more openly and honestly. However, they did not result in any progress.

✅ By December 1969 a further 60,000 troops were withdrawn from Vietnam. Cabot Lodge resigned after the final public peace talks did not lead to any progress.

✅ In February 1970, there were further secret meetings between Kissinger (p.104) and Le Duc.

✅ In April 1970, US forces launched a ground invasion of Cambodia and Nixon announced 150,000 troops would be required in Vietnam, prompting further protests in the USA.

✅ An invasion of Laos, led by the ARVN and supported by US military, was launched in February 1971.

✅ In January 1972, Nixon announced that Kissinger (p.104) had achieved a 'peace with honour' through secret negotiations with North Vietnam.

✅ Nixon undertook a symbolic visit to China in an attempt to improve relations in February 1972.

✅ North Vietnam carried out an attack on South Vietnam in March 1972. In retaliation, US forces bombed Hanoi in North Vietnam.

✅ In May 1972, Nixon visited the USSR to improve relations there, and to encourage the Soviets to pressure Ho Chi Minh (p.105) to end to the war.

✅ In October 1972 there was a significant turning point in negotiations in Paris.

✅ The Paris Peace Accord (p.94) was signed on 27th January, 1973.

☑ In March 1973, the last US soldiers left Vietnam.

What did Nixon promise to South Vietnam once the US had withdrawn?

While Nixon was committed to America's withdrawal from Vietnam, he still firmly believed in the Domino Theory In order to ensure South Vietnam did not fall to communism once the USA had left, he promised it support with mo and weapons.

What happened to South Vietnam after the US withdrew?

The following happened to South Vietnam once the final troops left in March 1973:

☑ The money and weapons promised by Nixon did not materialise. It was felt far too much money had been spent the war and the US government refused to send further support to what it saw as a corrupt and cruel regime.

☑ In December 1974, North Vietnam attacked the town of Phuoc Long in South Vietnam. This marked the beginnin an extensive campaign of attacks that saw the North Vietnamese occupy a number of cities and military bases.

☑ In April 1975 the capital city of South Vietnam, Saigon, fell to communism and was renamed Ho Chi Minh *(p.105)*

What were the consequences of US withdrawal from Vietnam?

There were 2 important consequences of American withdrawal from Vietnam:

☑ An end to the war after decades of conflict.

☑ After the fall of Saigon *(p.95)* in 1975, North and South Vietnam were united as a communist nation.

DID YOU KNOW?

The Vietnam War was America's longest war.

THE PARIS PEACE TALKS

'Now that we have achieved an honorable agreement, let us be proud that America did not settle for a peace that would have betrayed our allies.'
President Richard Nixon, 1973

What were the Paris Peace Accords?

The Paris Peace Accords were agreements to end the war and restore peace in Vietnam.

When were the Paris Peace Accords signed?

They were signed on 27th January, 1973.

Who were the key figures that negotiated the Paris Peace Accords?

The key figures involved in public and secret meetings where a peace agreement was negotiated were the USA's Hen Kissinger *(p.104)* and North Vietnam's Le Duc Tho.

Who signed the Paris Peace Accords?

There were 4 signatories to the Paris Accords:

☑ The USA.

☑ North Vietnam.

- ☑ South Vietnam.
- ☑ The National Liberation Front, otherwise known as the Vietcong *(p.58)*.

What were the agreements of the Paris Accords?

There were 7 agreements in the Paris Peace Accords:

- ☑ Acceptance of the reunification of Vietnam, and agreement a new government would be elected under international supervision.
- ☑ All four parties agreed to a ceasefire.
- ☑ Agreement to keep the armies of both Vietnamese governments, but the USA would not send aid to the ARVN.
- ☑ The USA would withdraw all troops, equipment and advisers within 60 days.
- ☑ All sides would exchange prisoners of war and equipment within 60 days.
- ☑ The USA would send aid for reconstruction to both sides.
- ☑ The USA government would not interfere in Vietnam in any way.

Was peace achieved with the Paris Accords?

The Paris Peace Accords did not bring instant peace.

DID YOU KNOW?

Henry Kissinger and Le Duc Tho received a Nobel Peace Prize in 1973 for their role in the Vietnam War peace negotiations.

THE FALL OF SAIGON

'It has been a long fight and we have lost... Let us hope that we will not have another Vietnam experience and that we have learned our lesson.'
Thomas Polgar, CIA Station Chief in Saigon

What was the fall of Saigon?

This was the capture of Saigon, the capital of South Vietnam, by the People's Army of Vietnam and the Vietcong *(p.58)*.

When was the fall of Saigon?

The fall of Saigon happened on 30th April, 1975.

What happened to US soldiers during the fall of Saigon?

The remaining US soldiers, and some Vietnamese refugees, were evacuated by helicopter.

What was the importance of the fall of Saigon?

The fall of Saigon was important for 2 reasons:

- ☑ It marked the end of the Vietnam War *(p.43)*.
- ☑ Vietnam became a united communist country.

THE REASONS FOR US FAILURE IN VIETNAM

There is a broad consensus among professional historians that the Vietnam War was effectively unwinnable.'
Historian Kevin Boylan

What caused the USA to fail in Vietnam?

The American government and public lacked a clear understanding of, or the motivation and adaptability to succee[...] Vietnam. They were also at a disadvantage culturally, politically and militarily, as they were not Vietnamese.

What were the main reasons the USA failed in Vietnam?

The 4 main reasons that contributed to the USA's failure in Vietnam were:

- ☑ The tactics and resolve of the Vietcong *(p.58)*.
- ☑ The cultural weaknesses of the USA in Vietnam.
- ☑ The political and public opposition to the war in the USA.
- ☑ The military weaknesses of the American forces.

Why did cultural weaknesses lead to the USA failing in Vietnam?

Cultural weakness was a key reason of the USA's failure in Vietnam due to the following:

- ☑ Many Americans had racist attitudes towards the Vietnamese, meaning they did not always treat local civilians [...] This led to atrocities like the My Lai Massacre *(p.75)*. US forces needed the support of the locals, but mostly aliena[...] them.
- ☑ It was hard to gain support from the locals because they didn't speak their language and needed interpreters.
- ☑ Most Americans had no idea what the country was like. They didn't understand why villagers were unwilling to [...] the lands where their ancestors were buried. This led to feelings of hatred from the local population and increas[...] support for the Vietcong *(p.58)*.
- ☑ The Americans didn't realise most Vietnamese villagers were unable to read, so dropping leaflets warning them [...] leave before bombing raids happened didn't work. Millions of innocent civilians were killed during the conflict.
- ☑ Many South Vietnamese saw the USA as occupiers imposing their ideas - just as the French and Japanese had - a[...] not advocates for democracy. They helped the Vietcong *(p.58)*, creating further difficulties for the US forces.

Why did political and public opposition lead to the USA's failure in Vietnam?

Political and public opposition led to the USA's failure in the Vietnam War *(p.43)* for the following reasons:

- ☑ The USA backed the South Vietnamese government, which was corrupt. Many officials had worked for the Fren[...] making America even more unpopular. Political figures and the American public objected to the USA fighting a [...] that defended a corrupt regime.
- ☑ The USA faced opposition at home in the form of anti-war protests, and restricted funding from Congress after [...] This placed President Nixon *(p.106)* under huge pressure to withdraw from Vietnam.
- ☑ The US public questioned the legitimacy of the war, meaning the US government no longer had a mandate to fig[...]

✅ Americans were horrified by media coverage of the war, and this led to a growth in the anti-war movement. By 1971, many surveys showed the majority of American people wanted US troops brought home immediately and an end to the conflict. The US government could not fight a war its people did not want.

Why did weaknesses in the USA's military lead to its failure in Vietnam?

Military weaknesses in the US forces led to failure in Vietnam for the following reasons:

✅ The military believed the war could be won with more troops and through bombing campaigns in North Vietnam, which was not the limited war the government wanted. US forces also failed to adjust their tactics to suit Vietnam's terrain and climate.

✅ US tactics alienated locals and caused resentment. 'Search and destroy (p.70)' included soldiers burning the homes of villagers.

✅ As the war progressed more soldiers were needed, so the draft became increasingly important. It meant many young and inexperienced soldiers were posted to Vietnam - and, as they returned home after a year, they left just as they were learning how to fight in the country's tough conditions. This contributed to the high number of casualties.

✅ Soldiers lacked training in how to combat guerrilla tactics. Their weapon and methods were ineffective in the jungle. One key problem faced by inexperienced GIs was the inability to recognise the enemy, leading to the deaths of innocent civilians and demoralised troops.

✅ Discipline among US soldiers was inadequate. Drug taking and desertion - where a soldier would leave his post - were rife. Approximately 30 per cent of US troops in Vietnam used heroin, further impacting their competency to fight effectively.

✅ The US military did not adapt their approach to combat the Vietcong's (p.58) guerrilla tactics, and therefore could not beat it.

✅ Their tactics often killed innocent civilians and sometimes their own troops. This led to low morale among the US forces which made it difficult for them to fight.

✅ With 12,000km between the USA and Vietnam, it meant US forces often had problems with their equipment and weapons.

✅ Racial inequalities in the US Army led to low morale and significant opposition back home. By 1970, black Americans made up 11 per cent of soldiers in Vietnam but almost 25 per cent of the casualties. Black soldiers questioned why they were fighting a war in the name of a freedom they did not have themselves.

How did the strengths of the Vietcong lead to the USA's failure in Vietnam?

The strength of both the Vietcong's (p.58) tactics and its resolve led to US failure in Vietnam for the following reasons:

✅ They knew the landscape, culture and language of the south, and so could easily navigate their way around undetected. They could also garner the support of the locals.

✅ The Vietnamese had a history of fighting foreign invaders, namely France and Japan. They were determined to remove all foreign influences from their country.

✅ The Vietcong (p.58) was already well established in the south, so North Vietnam could work with them and send supplies using the Ho Chi Minh Trail (p.59). Many North Vietnamese fighters were originally from the south, before the 1954 Geneva Accords, and so had family and contacts they could use.

✅ They had international support. Between 1954 and 1967, China and the USSR sent $3 billion in aid, weapons, and equipment. Laos and Cambodia allowed the Ho Chi Minh Trail (p.59) to run through their countries, and there was little America could do to stop this without further conflict.

✅ The North Vietnamese and Vietcong (p.58) troops were used to jungle conditions. They used guerrilla tactics and fought small skirmishes, although they could also fight large battles. These tactics were perfect for the terrain, and the USA could not fight effectively.

✅ The Vietcong (p.58) used a system of tunnels and bases to move supplies, troops and equipment. They were well-organised and experienced. The USA continuously failed at destroying the Vietcong's supply lines.

✅ The North Vietnamese and Vietcong (p.58) troops were fighting for their country. They had a clear motive to achieve victory and fought with fierce determination. The US troops, however, were fighting 12,000km from home for a cause they increasingly cared less about.

THE IMPACT OF THE VIETNAM WAR

'War is not combat, though combat is a part of war. Combatants are not the main participants in modern war. Modern war affects civilians far more and far longer than combatants.'
Nick Turse's article, 'The Intercept'

What was the impact of the Vietnam War?

The financial, human and environmental impact of the Vietnam War *(p.43)* was huge. It also had a major effect on the USA's reputation at home and abroad.

What was the financial impact of the Vietnam War?

The financial impact included:

- ☑ The war cost an estimated $170 billion - $1 trillion at today's rates.
- ☑ Long-term costs included benefits and pensions given to Vietnam veterans, or to their families if they died in serv It is thought these costs doubled the price of the war.
- ☑ Decades of conflict left Vietnam financially unstable and many people faced starvation as a result.

What was the significance of the financial impact of the Vietnam War?

The financial cost of the war meant promises of domestic reform in America were broken. Johnson *(p.102)* had promis a 'Great Society' and a 'War on Poverty'. However, with America spending billions of dollars every year on the Vietna War *(p.43)*, there was no money left for better education and healthcare.

What was the impact of the human cost of the Vietnam War?

The impact of the human cost of the war included:

- ☑ Approximately 58,000 American soldiers died. Their average age at death was 23.
- ☑ 300,000 US troops were injured.
- ☑ Returning soldiers were seen as the murderers of innocent people by opponents of the war, and as losers by those who had supported it. As a result they faced much negativity.
- ☑ Soldiers that did not have to live with physical disabilities caused by war injuries often suffered from mental heal problems due to drug addiction and the trauma they had experienced.
- ☑ It is estimated 1 million Vietnamese soldiers were killed during the conflict and a further 2 million wounded.
- ☑ Figures suggest 2 million Vietnamese civilians were killed, and 5 million injured.
- ☑ Many homes were destroyed during the conflict, leaving 11 million refugees. Many of these lived in poverty and turned to drug addiction and prostitution due to the influence of American culture.
- ☑ Many US soldiers had relationships with Vietnamese women, and approximately 100,000 children were born as a consequence. Around 3,000 children were taken from orphanages and hospitals and flown around the world to b adopted in 'Operation Babylift', but many were abandoned.
- ☑ The children born from relationships between American troops and local women had challenging lives. They were seen as different and a reminder of the horrors of the war. They suffered abuse and some were sold as labour.

Quizzes, amazing exam preparation tools and more at GCSEHistory.com

- [x] Many soldiers developed cancer and other illnesses due to the effects of chemical weapons like napalm and Agent Orange.
- [x] Even today, many Vietnamese people develop illnesses and disabilities as a result of traces of chemicals that remain in the soil.

What was the environmental impact of the Vietnam War?

The environmental cost of the Vietnam War included:

- [x] In one year alone, the use of Agent Orange destroyed 1 million hectares of forest in Vietnam.
- [x] 300,000 hectares of farmland was destroyed by chemicals dropped by US forces, making it unusable for food production.
- [x] 7 million tonnes of bombs were dropped, destroying roads, bridges and important irrigation systems.
- [x] There are still significant numbers of unexploded bombs across Vietnam.

What was the impact of the Vietnam War on America's reputation at home?

The Vietnam War (p.43) affected America's domestic reputation in a number of ways:

- [x] The war divided America. Many opposed it and felt America's actions were morally wrong. Others felt it was unpatriotic to question the government's actions and said anti-war protesters were traitors and communists.
- [x] The cover-up of events like My Lai, and Nixon's secret bombings of Cambodia, created a culture of distrust of the government.

What was the impact of the Vietnam War on America's reputation abroad?

The Vietnam War (p.43) impacted America's reputation abroad in the following ways:

- [x] America was mostly seen as the loser in the war as it failed to defeat the Vietcong (p.58). This was embarrassing for a nation that saw itself as a superpower.
- [x] America's actions were hypocritical. On one hand it proclaimed freedom and peace for all and claimed it was 'the land of the free'. On the other, unarmed protesters were being shot at; its soldiers carried out atrocities such as the My Lai Massacre (p.75); innocent civilians were killed and maimed through its use of chemical weapons.
- [x] America failed to contain communism in Southeast Asia. Vietnam, Cambodia and Laos all became communist states. This was a further embarrassment.

What was the impact of the war on Vietnam politically?

The war led to Vietnam becoming united under a communist government. However, it faced further hostility from the US government, which blocked its attempt to join the United Nations (p.25), leaving it internationally isolated.

DID YOU KNOW?

US soldiers, who had no option but to serve, came home to be branded 'baby killers'.

WALTER CRONKITE

Walter Cronkite was a journalist who played a key role in influencing public opinion.

Who was Walter Cronkite?

Walter Cronkite was an American news broadcaster who became known as 'the most trusted man in America' due reporting on the Vietnam War *(p.43)*.

What was Walter Cronkite's background?

Walter Cronkite's background included:

- ☑ He studied political science at the University of Texas.
- ☑ Cronkite's early career as a journalist saw him covering events during the Second World War and the Nurember trials.
- ☑ He joined CBS news in 1950, and became well known by the public.

What was significant about Walter Cronkite?

Cronkite's role as a journalist contributed to the growing opposition to the war, which played a part in the USA's withdrawal from Vietnam.

DID YOU KNOW?

Cronkite reported on many assassinations, including John F Kennedy's assassination, he also reported the news of both Martin Luther King, Jr., and John Lennon being killed.

NGO DINH DIEM

'Follow me if I advance! Kill me if I retreat! Revenge me if I die!'
Ngo Dinh Diem

Who was Ngo Dinh Diem?

Ngo Dinh Diem was the final prime minister of the State of Vietnam from 1954 to 1955, and then President of South Vietnam from 1955 to 1963.

What was Ngo Dinh Diem's background?

Diem was a Catholic, born in Vietnam. He worked for French officials from a young age.

What was Ngo Dinh Diem's relationship with Ho Chi Minh?

Ho Chi Minh's *(p.105)* forces captured Diem in 1945 and offered him a position in the new Democratic Republic of Vietnam. However, Diem was not interested and fled to the USA for ten years.

What influence did the USA have on Ngo Dinh Diem's life?

It was during his time in America that Diem met fellow Catholic, John F Kennedy *(p.103)*. Diem built a reputation as a potential leader of a future US-backed government in South Vietnam.

Was Diem a good president?

Diem was initially regarded as a good president. He built new schools and strengthened the economy. However, this changed because he increased his power, allowed corruption, and was anti-Buddhist.

Who supported Diem?

Diem had support from the USA, which was concerned the proposed 1956 elections would be won by the communists.

> **DID YOU KNOW?**
>
> The French hugely opposed the proposal to place Diem in charge in South Vietnam because, they said, he was 'not only incapable, but mad.'

PRESIDENT DWIGHT D EISENHOWER

'There is one thing about being president - nobody can tell you when to sit down.'
President Dwight Eisenhower

Who was President Eisenhower?

Dwight D Eisenhower was the 34th President of the United States.

When was Eisenhower president?

Eisenhower was President of the United States from 1953 until 1961.

What was President Eisenhower's background?

President Eisenhower's background included the following:

- ☑ Eisenhower was a member of the US armed forces throughout the 1920s and 1930s.
- ☑ He was a general in the army during the Second World War and was in charge of the D-Day landings in 1944.
- ☑ He became the supreme commander of NATO in December 1950.
- ☑ His war record helped him secure the presidency.

What were the key events of Eisenhower's presidency?

Some of the key events of Eisenhower's presidency included:

- ☑ In 1953 he helped negotiate an armistice that brought peace to Korea.
- ☑ He committed the USA to protecting South Vietnam from communism in 1953.
- ☑ He was in power during the Montgomery Bus Boycott, led by Rosa Parks, which lasted for twelve months between 1955 and 1956.
- ☑ In 1957 he signed the Civil Rights Act and set up a permanent Civil Rights Commission.

What were Eisenhower's beliefs about the Cold War?

Eisenhower was anti-communist and committed to the policy of containment. He articulated the concept of the 'Domino Theory *(p.50)*'.

PRESIDENT LYNDON B JOHNSON

'I want to build the kind of nation that President Roosevelt hoped for, President Truman worked for and President Kennedy died for.'
President Lyndon B Johnson, 1964

Who was President Johnson?

Lyndon B Johnson was the 36th President of the United States.

When was Johnson president?

Lyndon B Johnson was in office from 1963 to 1969.

What was Johnson's background?

Johnson's background included the following:

- He did not come from a wealthy background, and this shaped the kind of president he wanted to be.
- His ambitions as president included creating a 'Great Society' that was fair to everyone.
- Despite his ambitions he is most remembered for his role in the Vietnam War *(p. 43)*.

What were the key events in Johnson's presidency?

Some of the key events of Johnson's presidency included the following:

- He took over as president after the assassination of John F Kennedy *(p. 103)*.
- He signed the Civil Rights Act of 1964, which made discrimination based on race or colour, sex, religion or national origin illegal.
- Congress passed the Gulf of Tonkin Resolution *(p. 64)*, giving Johnson the power to pursue military action in Vietnam in August 1964.
- Martin Luther King Junior was assassinated in April 1968.
- The Tet Offensive *(p. 74)* happened in June 1968.

What were Johnson's views on the Cold War?

Johnson was anti-communist and, like Truman, Eisenhower and Kennedy *(p. 103)*, he was committed to stopping the spread of communism.

Quizzes, amazing exam preparation tools and more at GCSEHistory.com

PRESIDENT JOHN F KENNEDY

'... a great and good man.'
President Lyndon B Johnson, 1963

Who was President Kennedy?

John F Kennedy, commonly referred to as JFK, was the 35th President of the United States.

When was Kennedy president?

John F Kennedy was president between January 1961 and November 1963.

What was Kennedy's background?

Kennedy's background included the following:

- ☑ He came from an Irish-American family which was very wealthy and heavily involved in politics.
- ☑ He went to Harvard University and studied politics. He wrote his dissertation on Britain's policy of the appeasement of Adolf Hitler.
- ☑ He was in the US navy and served in the Second World War, where he was seriously injured when his boat was destroyed by the Japanese.

What were the key events of Kennedy's presidency?

The key events of Kennedy's presidency included the following:

- ☑ Kennedy created the Peace Corps in 1961.
- ☑ The Bay of Pigs Invasion in Cuba, in April 1961.
- ☑ In May 1961 he pledged America would put a man on the moon by the end of the decade.
- ☑ The Berlin Wall was built in 1961.
- ☑ The Cuban Missile Crisis took place in October 1962.
- ☑ He signed the Limited Nuclear Test Ban Treaty in August 1963.

What were Kennedy's beliefs about the Cold War?

Kennedy was anti-communist and, like his predecessors, was committed to containing communism. However, he was aware of the dangers of nuclear warfare after tensions were brought to the brink during the Cuban Missile Crisis, and wanted to reduce the chances of nuclear war.

What was President Kennedy's role in Vietnam?

President Kennedy continued to support South Vietnam with money, military advisers and commandos.

How did President Kennedy die?

Kennedy was assassinated in November 1963 in Dallas, Texas.

DID YOU KNOW?

Kennedy was the youngest ever president, elected at the age of 40, and the first Catholic president.

HENRY KISSINGER

'Kissinger brought peace to Vietnam the same way Napoleon brought peace to Europe: by losing.'
Author Joseph Heller, 1979

Who was Henry Kissinger?

Henry Kissinger was National Security Adviser to President Nixon *(p.106)*. He later became Secretary of State.

When was Henry Kissinger national security advisor?

He was National Security Advisor from 1969 to 1973.

What was Henry Kissinger's background?

There are 5 important points in Kissinger's background:

- ✅ He was born in Germany in 1923 to a Jewish family.
- ✅ His family emigrated to the USA in 1938 to escape Nazi persecution.
- ✅ He served in the US armed forces during the Second World War.
- ✅ He studied political science at Harvard University, where he began advising the US government on foreign polic
- ✅ Kissinger's ethos was common sense and practicality in politics.

What was significant about Henry Kissinger?

Kissinger was an incredibly skillful politician. He successfully negotiated the Paris Peace Agreement with North Vietnam's Le Duc Tho, ending the war in Vietnam in 1973. He won a Nobel Peace Prize for his role in the peace settlement.

DID YOU KNOW?

During the Second World War he worked in intelligence, translating classified German documents and messages.

GENERAL DOUGLAS MACARTHUR

You are remembered for the rules you break.'
General Douglas MacArthur

Who was General Douglas MacArthur?

General Douglas MacArthur was commander of the UN forces in Korea in 1950.

What was General Douglas MacArthur's background?

There are 3 important points to note:

- ✅ He was born into a family with a military background.
- ✅ He studied at the US Military Academy, West Point.
- ✅ He fought for the US armed forces in the First World War and was awarded 13 medals for bravery.
- ✅ He fought in the Second World War as the commander against Japan and played a leading role in rebuilding the country afterwards.

What was the significance of General Douglas MacArthur?

MacArthur was famed for being stubborn and arrogant. It was these personality traits that landed him in trouble with President Truman during the Korean War *(p.22)*, when he ignored orders and was subsequently fired.

> ### DID YOU KNOW?
>
> MacArthur vomited on the front steps of the White House when FDR proposed extensive military cuts in 1934.

HO CHI MINH

'You will kill ten of us, we will kill one of you, but in the end, you will tire of it first.'
Ho Chi Minh, 1946

Who was Ho Chi Minh?

Ho Chi Minh was the communist leader of North Vietnam.

What were Ho Chi Minh's main aims?

Ho Chi Minh's main aim was to achieve a communist, united, and independent Vietnam.

What were Ho Chi Minh's achievements?

Ho Chi Minh had 8 main achievements including:

- ☑ He founded the Vietminh *(p.46)*.
- ☑ He led the Vietnamese to victory over the Japanese and the French, and played a major role in the war against the US.
- ☑ He helped communism to develop in Vietnam.
- ☑ He was instrumental in the development of the Ho Chi Minh Trail *(p.59)*.
- ☑ He was prime minister of North Vietnam from 1945 to 1955.
- ☑ He was president of North Vietnam from 1945 to 1969.
- ☑ He created the North Vietnamese Army and the Vietcong *(p.58)*.
- ☑ He established links with China and the USSR.

What was Ho Chi Minh's link to the Vietcong?

He was instrumental in the creation of the Vietcong *(p.58)* by encouraging the different armed groups in the south to work together as one organisation. The new organisation became known as the National Liberation Front in December 1960. In the south they were called the 'Vietcong' which meant Vietnamese communist.

> ### DID YOU KNOW?
>
> Ho Chi Minh changed his name in the 1940s - it means 'Bringer of Light'.

PRESIDENT RICHARD NIXON

'A man is not finished when he's defeated. He's finished when he quits.'
President Richard Nixon, 1969

Who was Richard Nixon?

Richard Nixon was the 37th President of the United States of America.

When was Nixon president?

Nixon was President of the United States from 1969 until 1974.

What was Nixon's background?

Nixon's background included the following:

- ☑ He was a very successful student and studied law at university.
- ☑ He served in the US navy during the Second World War.
- ☑ He served as Eisenhower's vice-president between 1953 and 1961.
- ☑ He ran against John F Kennedy *(p.103)* in the 1960 presidential election and lost.

What were the key events in Nixon's presidency?

The key events in Nixon's presidency included:

- ☑ In May 1964, he made a commitment to withdraw the USA from Vietnam.
- ☑ In February 1972, he visited China and was the first US president to visit the communist state.
- ☑ In May 1972, he visited the USSR.
- ☑ In June 1972, the Watergate *(p.90)* scandal began.
- ☑ In January 1973, the Paris Peace Accords were signed, signalling an end to the Vietnam War *(p.43)*.
- ☑ In June 1973, he took responsibility for the Watergate *(p.90)* scandal.
- ☑ He faced charges of impeachment in July 1974.
- ☑ He became the first US president to resign from office in August 1974.

What were Nixon's views on the Cold War?

Nixon was anti-communist and committed to the policy of containment. However, he also took office at a time when America's Cold War-related *(p.16)* spending had reached an unsustainable high. He looked at reducing tensions with communist states, including the USSR and China, to reduce spending.

Why was Nixon elected president?

One of the key reasons why Nixon was elected president in 1969 was because of President Johnson's *(p.102)* failures in Vietnam War *(p.43)*.

Why did Nixon resign as president of the USA?

Richard Nixon resigned as president of the USA on 9th August, 1974 because of his involvement in the Watergate *(p.9* Scandal.

DID YOU KNOW?

Richard Nixon applied to join the FBI in the 1930s, but never heard back from the organisation.

Quizzes, amazing exam preparation tools and more at GCSEHistory.com

SYNGMAN RHEE

Syngman Rhee was the US-backed president of South Korea.

Who was Syngman Rhee?

Syngman Rhee was a Korean politician who led the country of South Korea. He was born in March 1875, and died in July 1965.

When was Syngman Rhee leader of South Korea?

Rhee was leader of South Korea from 1948 to 1965.

What was Syngman Rhee's background?

Syngman Rhee's background included the following:

- ☑ He was sent to prison in 1897 for opposing the Korean royal family.
- ☑ When Rhee was released from prison he moved to the USA to study as a lawyer.
- ☑ In 1919 he was elected President of Korea. However, he did not take up the role, as Japan controlled Korea and Rhee was exiled.
- ☑ In 1948 he became the first President of South Korea. He had a reputation as a brutal ruler.

What was significant about Syngman Rhee?

Rhee was the first leader of South Korea, and ruled during the Korean War *(p.22)*.

DID YOU KNOW?

Rhee wrote a book called 'Japan Inside Out', predicting Japanese aggression towards the USA.

KIM IL-SUNG

'The oppressed peoples can liberate themselves only through struggle. This is a simple truth confirmed by history.'
Kim Il Sung

Who was Kim Il-Sung?

Kim Il-Sung was a politician who led North Korea. He was born in April 1912 and died in July 1994.

When was Kim Il-Sung leader of North Korea?

He was leader of North Korea from 1948 to 1994.

What was Kim Il-Sung's background?

Kim Il-Sung's background included the following:

- ☑ He created the Young Communist League of Korea in 1927.
- ☑ He led a group that fought against the Japanese during their years of rule.
- ☑ He was a major in the Soviet army and fought for the USSR during the Second World War.

- ☑ In 1945 he formed the Communist Party of North Korea.
- ☑ He became leader of North Korea in 1948 and ruled until his death in 1994.
- ☑ With Stalin's permission he began a military campaign to unite Korea, after its division at the end of the Second World War. This resulted in war starting in 1950.

What was the significance of Kim II-Sung?

Kim II-Sung was significant because of his role in causing the Korean War *(p.22)*. He launched an invasion of South in order to unite the two nations.

DID YOU KNOW?

Kim II-Sung was the absolute ruler of North Korea for 46 years.

PRESIDENT HARRY TRUMAN

'Never step on a fresh turd on a hot summer's day. The buck stops here!'
President Truman

Who was President Truman?

Harry S Truman was the 33rd President of the United States, holding office from 1945 to 1953.

What was an overview of Truman's time as president?

Truman's time as president included the following events:

- ☑ He took over from Franklin D Roosevelt during the Second World War.
- ☑ He oversaw huge challenges both domestically and internationally as America transitioned from fighting the Se World War in 1945 to the onset of the Cold War *(p.16)* between 1947 and 1949.
- ☑ His policy of the Truman Doctrine *(p.19)* and the policy of the containment became the cornerstone of American foreign policy for decades.
- ☑ In the years after his presidency he faced huge criticism as the president who 'lost China to communism'.
- ☑ He is now considered by historians to be one of America's greatest presidents.

What was President Truman's attitude towards communism?

Truman objected to the USSR's control over the countries of eastern Europe. He believed the USSR was determined expand, so he sought to contain the spread of communism during his time in office.

What was Truman's involvement in the Cold War?

The Truman Doctrine *(p.19)*, in 1947, highlighted America's new stance on communism, and signalled the beginning the US policy of containment.

DID YOU KNOW?

Truman was the only president in the 1900s who did not attend college.

---

gression - angry, hostile or violent behaviour displayed without vocation.

iculture - an umbrella term to do with farming, growing crops raising animals.

ance - a union between groups or countries that benefits each mber.

es - parties working together for a common objective, such as ntries involved in a war. In both world wars, 'Allies' refers to se countries on the side of Great Britain.

munition - collective term given to bullets and shells.

putate, Amputation - to surgically remove a limb from neone's body.

nistice - an agreement between two or more opposing sides in ar to stop fighting.

illery - large guns used in warfare.

assinate - to murder someone, usually an important figure, en for religious or political reasons.

assination - the act of murdering someone, usually an portant person.

rition - the act of wearing down an enemy until they collapse ough continued attacks.

oby traps - seemingly harmless devices concealing something t will kill, harm or surprise. Especially in warfare, booby traps re often set off by a wire and contained explosives.

ycott - a way of protesting or bringing about change by refusing buy something or use services.

be, Bribery, Bribes - to dishonestly persuade someone to do nething for you in return for money or other inducements.

ffer - a protective barrier.

mpaign - a political movement to get something changed; in litary terms, it refers to a series of operations to achieve a goal.

pitalism - the idea of goods and services being exchanged for ney, private ownership of property and businesses, and ceptance of a hierarchical society.

sualties - people who have been injured or killed, such as ring a war, accident or catastrophe.

tholic - a Christian who belongs to the Roman Catholic Church.

asefire - when the various sides involved in conflict agree to p fighting.

nsorship - the control of information in the media by a vernment, whereby information considered obscene or acceptable is suppressed.

Civil rights - the rights a citizen has to political or social freedoms, such as the right to vote or freedom of speech.

Civilian - a non-military person.

Claim - someone's assertion of their right to something - for example, a claim to the throne.

Colonies, Colony - a country or area controlled by another country and occupied by settlers.

Communism - the belief, based on the ideas of Karl Marx, that all people should be equal in society without government, money or private property. Everything is owned by by the people, and each person receives according to need.

Communist - a believer in communism.

Conference - a formal meeting to discuss common issues of interest or concern.

Conscription - mandatory enlistment of people into a state service, usually the military.

Containment - meaning to keep something under control or within limits, it often refers to the American idea of stopping the spread of communism.

Cooperate, Cooperation - to work together to achieve a common aim. Frequently used in relation to politics, economics or law.

Corrupt - when someone is willing to act dishonestly for their own personal gain.

Coup - a sudden, violent and illegal overthrow of the government by a small group - for example, the chiefs of an army.

Culture - the ideas, customs, and social behaviour of a particular people or society.

D

Deadlock - a situation where no action can be taken and neither side can make progress against the other; effectively a draw.

Defect - the act of defection; to leave your country or cause for another.

Demilitarised - to remove all military forces from an area and forbid them to be stationed there.

Democracy - a political system where a population votes for its government on a regular basis. The word is Greek for 'the rule of people' or 'people power'.

Democratic - relating to or supporting the principles of democracy.

Deploy - to move military troops or equipment into position or a place so they are ready for action.

Discriminate, Discrimination - to treat a person or group of people differently and in an unfair way.

Dispute - a disagreement or argument; often used to describe conflict between different countries.

Doctrine - a stated principle of government policy; can also refer to a set of beliefs held and taught by a church, political party or other group.

Domino Theory - a popular idea during the Cold War that suggested if one country became communist, others nearby would follow suit.

Détente - the easing of tension, especially between two countries.

E

Economic - relating to the economy; also used when justifying something in terms of profitability.

Economy - a country, state or region's position in terms of production and consumption of goods and services, and the supply of money.

Electorate - a group of people who are eligible to vote.

Embassy - historically, a deputation sent by one ruler, state or country to another. More recently, it is also the accepted name for the official residence or offices of an ambassador.

Empire - a group of states or countries ruled over and controlled by a single monarch.

Exile - to be banned from one's original country, usually as a punishment or for political reasons.

Export - to transport goods for sale to another country.

F

Fatalities, Fatality - Deaths.

Foreign policy - a government's strategy for dealing with other nations.

Free elections - elections in which voters are free to vote without interference.

Front - in war, the area where fighting is taking place.

G

GDP, Gross domestic product - the total annual value of a country's goods and services.

Guerrilla tactics, Guerrilla warfare - a way of fighting that typically involves hit-and-run style tactics.

Guerrillas - groups of small, independent fighters usually involved in a war against larger, regular military forces.

H

Harvest - the process of gathering and collecting crops.

Hippies - Groups of Americans who 'dropped out' of traditional life. Most did not go to college or work and travelled around the country, organising music festivals and protests against the Vietnam war and campaigning for world peace.

I

Ideology - a set of ideas and ideals, particularly around political ideas or economic policy, often shared by a group of people.

Impeach, Impeachment - to charge someone, usually a

high-ranking government official, with treason or a crime against the state.

Imperial, Imperialisation, Imperialism, Imperialist - is the practice or policy of taking possession of, and extending political and economic control over other areas or territories. Imperialism always requires the use of military, political or economic power of a stronger nation over that of a weaker one. An imperialist is someone who supports or practices imperialism and imperialism relates to a system of empire, for example the British Empire.

Independence, Independent - to be free of control, often meaning by another country, allowing the people of a nation the ability to govern themselves.

Industrial - related to industry, manufacturing and/or production.

Industry - the part of the economy concerned with turning raw materials into into manufactured goods, for example making furniture from wood.

Infrastructure - the basic physical and organisational facilities a society or country needs to function, such as transport networks, communications and power.

Intercontinental ballistic missile - a guided ballistic missile with a minimum range of 5,500km or 3,400 miles.

International relations - the relationships between different countries.

L

Left wing - used to describe political groups or individuals with beliefs that are usually centered around socialism and the idea of reform.

Legislation - a term for laws when they are considered collectively, for example housing legislation.

Legitimacy, Legitimate - accepted by law or conforming to the rules; can be defended as valid.

Limb - an arm or leg.

M

Mandate - authority to carry out a policy.

Mass - an act of worship in the Catholic Church.

Massacre - the deliberate and brutal slaughter of many people.

Mercenary - someone who takes action in order to earn money rather than out of principle.

Middle class - refers to the socio-economic group which includes people who are educated and have professional jobs, such as teachers or lawyers.

Military force - the use of armed forces.

Militia - an army created from the general population.

Mine - an explosive device usually hidden underground or underwater.

Minister - a senior member of government, usually responsible for a particular area such as education or finance.

k - a member of a religious community, often living a simple
f poverty, chastity and work.

ale - general mood of a group of people.

als - a person's set of rules about what they consider right and
ng, used to guide their actions and behaviour.

ass - an area of swampy or very wet and muddy ground which
fficult to cross.

alm - a petrol based chemical, used to devastating effect in
lict as it sticks to skin and causes terrible burns.

onalism, Nationalist, Nationalistic - identifying with your
nation and supporting its interests, often to the detriment or
sion of other nations.

otism - the practice of people in power favouring friends and
ly, often by giving them jobs or influence. Historically, this
especially common in government and the Church.

upation - the action, state or period when somewhere is taken
and occupied by a military force.

nsive - another way of saying an attack or campaign.

V, Prisoner of war, Prisoners of war - somebody who has been
ured and taken prisoner by enemy forces.

fication - Making something, or someone, peaceful.

iament - a group of politicians who make the laws of their
ntry, usually elected by the population.

sant - a poor farmer.

secution - hostility towards or harassment of someone, usually
to their race, religion or political beliefs.

netic Alphabet - A series of code words to indicate different
rs of the alphabet, E.G 'Alpha' to mean 'A'.

- a vote or survey.

ulation - the number of people who live in a specified place.

erty - the state of being extremely poor.

decessor - the person who came before; the previous person to
a role or position.

sident - the elected head of state of a republic.

vent, Preventative, Preventive - steps taken to stop something
n happening.

duction - a term used to describe how much of something is
le, for example saying a factory has a high production rate.

paganda - biased information aimed at persuading people to
nk a certain way.

Prosecute - to institute or conduct legal proceedings against a
person or organisation.

Proxy war - a conflict between two sides acting on behalf of other
parties who are not directly involved, but who have usually
supplied equipment, arms and/or money.

Psychological - referring to a person's mental or emotional state.

Q

Quagmire - an area of swampy or very wet and muddy ground
which is difficult to cross.

R

Raid - a quick surprise attack on the enemy.

Rallies, Rally - a political event with speakers and a crowd,
designed to increase support for a politician, political party or an
idea.

Rational - when something is based on reason or logic, like
science.

Rebels - people who rise in opposition or armed resistance against
an established government or leader.

Reform, Reforming - change, usually in order to improve an
institution or practice.

Refugee, Refugees - a person who has been forced to leave where
they live due to war, disaster or persecution.

Restoration - to return something to its former owner, place or
condition; this includes returning a monarch to the throne or a
head of state to government.

Revolution - the forced overthrow of a government or social
system by its own people.

Rig, Rigged - politically, to interfere in or fix an election to
determine the winner.

S

Sanctions - actions taken against states who break international
laws, such as a refusal to trade with them or supply necessary
commodities.

Satellite state - a country under the control of another, such as
countries under USSR control during the Cold War.

Scandal, Scandalous - something that angers or shocks people
because rules or accepted standards of behaviour have been
broken.

Search and destroy, Seek and destroy - a tactic used by the US in
Vietnam. Helicopters brought in soldiers who searched out the
enemy in a specific area, such as a village, destroyed them, and
then left.

Sino - is a a reference to China or something relating to China. It is
a prefix which is used instead of China.

Soviet - an elected workers' council at local, regional or national
level in the former Soviet Union. It can also be a reference to the
Soviet Union or the USSR.

Stalemate - a situation where no action can be taken and neither side can make progress against the other; effectively a draw.

State, States - an area of land or a territory ruled by one government.

Strategy - a plan of action outlining how a goal will be achieved.

Strike - a refusal by employees to work as a form of protest, usually to bring about change in their working conditions. It puts pressure on their employer, who cannot run the business without workers.

Submission, Submit - a formal surrender and acceptance of a new authority.

Superior - better or higher in rank, status or quality.

T

Tactic - a strategy or method of achieving a goal.

Terrain - a stretch of land and usually used to refer to its physical features, eg mountainous, jungle etc.

Territories, Territory - an area of land under the control of a ruler/ country.

Treaty - a formal agreement, signed and ratified by two or more parties.

V

Veteran, Veterans - an ex-soldier.

Veto - the right to reject a decision or proposal.

Quizzes, amazing exam preparation tools and more at GCSEHistory.com